Stephen Nell

SPRINGBOK GLORY

TAFELBERG

Tafelberg,
an imprint of NB Publishers, a division of Media24 Boeke (Pty) Ltd,
40 Heerengracht, Cape Town, South Africa
PO Box 6525, Roggebaai, 8012, South Africa
www.tafelberg.com

Cover design: Doret Ferreira
Book design: Nazli Jacobs
E-book design: Nielfa Cassiem-Carelse

Editing: Greg Evans
Proofreading: Julie Miller
E-book checking: Lorraine Braid

Printed and bound in Paarl Media Paarl
Jan van Riebeeck Drive, Paarl, South Africa

First edition, first impression 2013
ISBN: 978-0-624-05742-0
(Epub) 978-0-624-05743-7
(Mobi) 978-0-624-06449-7

Dedicated to my big rugby mate,
Mveleli 'Thangana' Ncula

Table of Contents

Foreword

Stephen Nell and I met for the first time when I joined the Stormers and Western Province as a player in 2000.

We spent some time together in the ensuing years when he assisted me as a ghost writer for my column in the *Cape Times*. As time went by, he gained an understanding of how I thought about rugby and our working relationship became an absolute pleasure, and what is more, we became friends. That is why I was quite excited about this project because it has been written by a friend rather than simply a journalist.

Nevertheless, I'm happy that my friend has done the journalist in him justice.

I have a lot of respect for the media in general, but sometimes coaches and players find it amazing to see how wrong journalists can get things by observing from the outside.

What makes this book special to me is that a journalist has not merely looked at something from the outside and pretended to have all the answers. He actually went to speak to the people who were involved. As someone who was involved in many of the games and situations that are written about here, it brought back so many amazing memories because I experienced it exactly the way it is written.

Of course, there were several chapters where I wasn't involved first hand, but the views of players and coaches of previous generations are so relevant to today. Some things never change.

What I also like is that there are numerous voices in the book.

When you read an autobiography, you get one person's perspective. But when you blend the voices of coaches, players, administrators and selectors, you realise how different the facts are.

Having experienced rugby as a player and coach, I could read the book through the eyes of both. The fact that both experiences are incorporated is something the reader will find really interesting.

The chapter that brought back the most memories was the one on the World Cup of 1995. It's something I haven't talked or thought about a lot since and the memories came flooding back as I read it. To me that chapter had more value in stirring my emotions than the movie *Invictus*.

Stephen did not shy away from the spiritual aspect of our experience as players. Whether you like it or not, people are spiritual beings and it's very relevant within the South African rugby community and, in fact, world-wide. So many sports people get their strength from a belief in God.

I know that Stephen deliberately steered away from controversy, which is often a selling point for books. What is written here is interesting and engaging enough to sell on its merits. It's simply about some of South Africa's greatest test matches in the post-isolation phase and you'll feel better after reading it.

Politics, of course, is part of sport and particularly so in a complex society like South Africa. The interaction of politics with Springbok rugby is included here for context and I believe will enhance your understanding of the significance of some matches.

I mostly enjoyed the book because it's about emotions. That is, after all, what we recall when we look back on rugby matches and it's what the reader will experience when he hears every person speak.

You'll get a few fresh angles and experience things through the eyes of people who were at the coalface. Above all, you'll feel good when you put it down.

BRENDAN VENTER*

May 2013

* Brendan Venter lives in the Strand, where he has a medical practice and is a dedicated family man. At the time of writing he had just been appointed as Director of Rugby at the Sharks, held the position of technical director at English glamour club Saracens and was an assistant coach of the SA under-20 team. He played 24 matches for the Springboks, of which 17 were tests and represented South Africa at the Rugby World Cup tournaments of 1995 and 1999. He previously held the position of Director of Rugby at both London Irish and Saracens for two years, and was an assistant coach at the Stormers for two seasons.

Preface

It was a cold day in Edinburgh in November 2012 when I told Springbok coach Heyneke Meyer while exchanging pleasantries next to the training field off Peffermill Road that I regretted not packing a scarf for the end-of-season tour.

I resolved to purchase some winter essentials as soon as I returned to the team hotel on the Royal Mile but, as it turned out, this wasn't necessary.

There was a knock on my door and Springbok media manager De Jongh Borchardt presented me with a little gift. "This is from Heyneke," he said as he handed me a plastic packet with a Springbok scarf, beanie and blanket.

Knowing Meyer, it wasn't about buying good publicity. He was just being the nice guy that he is and I accepted it in that spirit. I certainly didn't consider it as a so-called "freebie" that journalists are strongly discouraged from taking. Those items are among my treasured keepsakes.

That little story captures my experience of covering Springbok rugby over several seasons. While the game may be fraught with politics, the team and its management have mostly remained true to the best traditions and values of what they represent.

My different experiences – the game's interaction with politics, the drama, the ecstasy and the agony – have prompted me to write about some of the Springboks' most significant matches and the context in which they were played. The period that I will cover is the post-isolation phase from 1992 onwards.

Much of what you will read you may already know from following the press and reading autobiographies. Nevertheless, I hope that some new interviews with key role-players and a slightly different approach will result in a pleasant reading experience and will also be informative.

You certainly won't be reading interviews with Francois Pienaar or Morné du Plessis about what the World Cup experience was like in 1995. And I specifically didn't choose the picture of Joel Stransky's drop goal or one featuring Nelson Mandela and Pienaar.

One of the challenges was finding something new regarding that incredible episode in South African rugby history. For that purpose I sat down with former Springbok midfielder Brendan Venter and quizzed him about the intervention he led when coach Kitch Christie produced a game plan that caused the players to have reservations about going into the final against the All Blacks.

Our discussion also moved into the spiritual realm and the outcome was a piece in which none of Pienaar, Stransky, Christie or even Nelson Mandela stood out as the biggest hero.

The chapter may well be derided, but the strong spiritual base of many South African players is an inseparable part of their experience of and grounding in the game.

I enjoyed sitting down with Nick Mallett to talk about the highlights of his tenure as Springbok coach – among others a magnificent victory over France at the Parc des Princes in Paris and some memorable wins over the All Blacks.

Jake White shared how he brought respectability back to Springbok rugby from 2004 onwards and shared the perils of his journey. John Smit, who skippered the side from 2004 through to 2011, also gave an in-depth interview.

Former Springbok assistant coach Gary Gold was very helpful in providing some insights into matches in the era from 2008 through to 2011, while Meyer also agreed to talk a little about the steady development of his side in 2012.

Notwithstanding the fact that such a book is all about covering old territory, I hope there are times when you will get a sense of what happened behind the scenes and how the drama unfolded.

Rugby's interaction with politics at large has always interested me and a few of the chapters are cast against that background. Along the way I also gained new insight into Mandela's immense impact on Springbok rugby.

If I have succeeded in my goal, the book will be mostly easy-reading, intriguing and uplifting.

The seed for the book was already planted in 2009 and it started as a project to write about matches between the Springboks and All Blacks from 1992 onwards. But "Rugby's Greatest Rivalry" is a topic that had been done to death and I decided not to go through with it.

By then I had already interviewed the likes of the late South African rugby supremo Louis Luyt, Danie Gerber, Joel Stransky and former All Black scrumhalf Ant Strachan.

Others who have helped me and to whom I am very grateful are Hannes Marais, Hennie le Roux, Brendan Venter, Chester Williams, Nick Mallett, Pieter Rossouw, Robbie Fleck, Jake White, Marius Joubert, John Smit, Bryan Habana, Gary Gold, Schalk Brits, Francois Louw, Heyneke Meyer and Tim Noakes.

The majority of the aforementioned had been criticised by me during their careers as players and coaches – sometimes harshly – but they were still willing to grant me an audience and were generous with their time.

Thanks also to Tim du Plessis and Chris Whitfield for granting me permission to lift the odd passage from *Die Burger* and the *Cape Times*, respectively. I had written most of those extracts for the newspapers, but copyright resides with the media houses. I also want to thank Tafelberg for the faith they had in me in publishing this book. Annie de Beer's assistance and patience are sincerely appreciated.

If there is something I realised from writing this book, it's that we as journalists and the public do not always treat our players and coaches with the respect they deserve.

Yes, the game is professional and they get paid the big bucks, but without exception they are there to make a difference and serve South African rugby. To that end this project was an education.

On the subject of education, I would like to thank Brendan Venter for being an inspiration and teaching me so much about the game. There were times that his leadership extended into other areas of my life.

His opinion is valued and I'm not the only one who thinks that. It also had a significant influence on South Africa's big moments during the World Cup campaigns of 1995 and 1999.

It is such moments that are celebrated and analysed in these pages. I hope you find it as enjoyable to read as I did to write.

STEPHEN NELL

30 April 2013

CHAPTER 1

No Longer All Black

*"It was a shame for Naas and Danie that they did not play much
football between 1981 and their return."*
– ANT STRACHAN

The doors of international competition finally swung open for the Springboks when a unity agreement was reached between the pre-democracy
national rugby bodies early in 1992.

No longer – officially at least – would race be a barrier to selection.

That's all the African National Congress (ANC) and international rugby
community wanted to know.

The newly-formed South African Rugby Football Union (Sarfu) wouldn't
have to wait for the country to go to the polls to embark on its journey.

History will show that they were probably a little too cavalier as matches
against New Zealand and world champions Australia were lined up on
successive Saturdays.

But it would certainly satisfy the hunger for serious competition.

In the romantic sense it was appropriate that the Springboks' first game
would be against the All Blacks.

It was the match South Africans and the rugby world wanted to see
above all else as it pitted rugby's greatest rivals against one another for
the first time since the controversial series in New Zealand in 1981.

South Africa did play the New Zealand Cavaliers in a home series in
1986, but it was not a representative side and, if anything, it was akin to the

Rebel cricket tours. It just created more illusions and frustrated positive change.

But here we were at last: the Springboks would return with a test against the All Blacks on 15 August 1992. South Africa would be coached by John Williams.

Interestingly, the plans for South Africa's first game had initially been very different.

Louis Luyt, a forceful man who was then president of the Transvaal Rugby Union (TRU), recalls that Danie Craven, in his capacity as joint-chairman of the unified South African Rugby Football Union (Sarfu), had given his word to Australian Rugby Union president Joe French that the first game would be against world champions, the Wallabies.

"I wanted the game to be played at Ellis Park, but Doc Craven considered Newlands the sanctum of rugby," Luyt recalled in an interview a few years before his passing.

"I asked Joe French whether they would consider playing a second game. He said two games were out of the question, but suggested I call New Zealand. They immediately agreed on condition that it was the first game.

Craven, regarded as South Africa's Mr Rugby, was among those who were concerned by the Springboks acting contrary to the art of war and storming into unfamiliar terrain.

"When we were allowed back, Doc Craven warned us about tackling the big nations too early. He warned us not to try to punch above our weight," said Luyt.

"I believe we should have beaten New Zealand that day. We very nearly did. If Pieter Müller had passed to James Small we would have scored a try under the posts that would have clinched the game. We were, of course, taken to the cleaners against Australia the following week."

But it was a simplistic way of looking at a game in which South Africa were clearly second best. The scoreline of 24-27 did not reflect how well they had, in fact, been beaten.

Should we really have expected anything else? While still capable of producing world class performances, South Africa's legendary duo of fly-half Naas Botha and outside centre Danie Gerber were both 34 years old.

Eighthman Jannie Breedt was very much in the same boat at 33.

These players were clearly deep into the twilight of their careers, but their presence was crucial as New Zealand rocked up with a side captained by hooker Sean Fitzpatrick and containing the likes of Michael Jones, Zinzan Brooke, Grant Fox, Frank Bunce and John Kirwan.

South Africa, on the other hand, were fielding a starting line-up with eight debutants in tighthead prop Lood Muller, lock Adri Geldenhuys, flank Ian Macdonald, scrumhalf Robert du Preez, left wing Pieter Hendriks, inside centre Pieter Müller, right wing James Small and fullback Theo van Rensburg.

Apart from a lack of test experience, there was the issue of trends in the game having passed South Africa by during their years of isolation.

And the tries they conceded exposed them.

Brooke first caught them with a sucker punch as he raced through from a tap penalty with a number of Springbok backs still turned.

While Botha opened South Africa's account with a penalty five minutes into the second half after they had been down 0-10 at half-time, there wouldn't be any respite.

Du Preez would learn a harsh lesson when he kicked the ball down the throat of Inga Tuigamala. The All Black left wing gave a few Springboks the runaround before Bunce broke superbly between Botha and Müller to set up Kirwan for the try. Fox then added a penalty to give the All Blacks a lead of 20-3.

But then came a Springbok fightback that featured two delightful tries by Gerber that sent a boorish crowd home satisfied.

The first try was made possible by Hendriks. He drew the defence before passing to Gerber, who in turn dummied All Black fullback John Timu before cutting inside and scoring. It was vintage Gerber.

Unfortunately the next score belonged to Timu himself, finishing after the All Black forwards had driven the ball up relentlessly before it travelled down the line on the open side.

Fox converted from the right-hand touchline and the All Blacks' lead was 27-10 with the match winding down.

The potential for humiliation was there but, as befitting their jersey, the Springboks would not go down without a fight and they scored two tries in the final face-saving five minutes.

Müller scored his try thanks to some good build-up play from a line-out deep in Kiwi territory before Gerber sent the crowd into delirium in the dying embers.

The legendary centre's second try highlighted Botha's astute decision-making and tactical nous. He made a vital switch in direction before Müller drew his man and found Gerber with a deft pass. Gerber again beat the last defender by cutting inside and scoring at virtually the same spot as for his first try.

Referee Sandy MacNeill blew his final whistle straight after Botha's conversion. The score was New Zealand 27, South Africa 24.

South Africa could point to missed opportunities – Small lost the ball with the try-line at his mercy and Müller could have put Van Rensburg away.

But the All Blacks built a cushion and would only look second best once they were effectively sure of the victory.

One of the key differences was that the All Blacks used their opportunities. South Africa failed to do so and clearly didn't have the composure for matches like these.

Significantly, however, the Boks had made a statement.

The match highlighted what a tragedy it was that two of South African rugby's greatest players of their era, in the figures of Botha and Gerber, didn't have the opportunity of lengthy test careers.

Having missed out on the Rugby World Cup tournaments of 1987 and 1991, they were clearly too old to make it to the World Cup in 1995.

The positive aspect was that a new generation was clearly coming to the fore. Müller had been particularly prominent in the first game back in international competition and he was one of a handful of Boks who would go on to much bigger and better things.

He would feature as South Africa clinched the Tri-Nations title in 1998, which included the first test victory on New Zealand soil at Athletic Park in Wellington since the tour of 1981. It happened to be at the same venue.

Small would end up a World Cup winner in 1995.

Left wing Pieter Hendriks would also etch his name into the Springbok annals with the manner in which he beat legendary Wallaby wing David Campese in South Africa's opening game at the tournament.

His suspension for involvement in a flare-up in the 1995 World Cup match against Canada in Port Elizabeth would also open the door for Chester Williams to re-enter the picture after injury had initially ruled him out of the tournament.

Hennie le Roux was an unused substitute in the first game back and would eventually partner Japie Mulder in midfield as the Springboks beat the All Blacks in the 1995 World Cup final.

But in many ways this match highlighted the years that had passed South Africa by. Gerber was still at the top of his game after he had been written off and Botha displayed tactical nous in spite of two missed penalties.

How good might they have been had it not been for isolation?

Botha himself was philosophical when questioned about the matter once, pointing to players across the racial spectrum that did not have the same opportunities.

Gerber had not even been in South Africa's initial plans and recalls the circumstances surrounding his inclusion.

"I was playing well on the wing at Western Province and nobody gave me a chance. The mentality seemed to be that when you are 30 you should be in a wheelchair. I was not picked in the initial squad, but Brendan Venter broke his leg. I was then called up and everything went well," he said.

"I could actually have scored four tries. I was stopped just short on one occasion and on another there was a forward pass from Pieter Müller. But two tries were enough after all the criticism that I was too old! I still went on tour to France and England after that and scored some tries there."

Fitzpatrick praised the Springboks when interviewed on television straight after the game.

"All credit to the Springboks. They came back at us. It's all looking good for them. I'm just glad we got them out of the way first because they are obviously going to build on it," he said.

"We applied pressure in the first half and the points came. Thankfully, in the second half early on, we applied more pressure and got further reward.

"But all credit to the Springboks. It was a mighty fine effort by them.

"There were a few anxious moments in the end. They said Danie Gerber was too old, but he'd do in any team of mine if he scored two tries like that!"

While All Black scrumhalf Ant Strachan didn't believe the game to be in doubt, he also credited the Springboks for their performance.

Furthermore, he did not share the view that South Africa necessarily would have been best-served approaching their return from isolation more conservatively against lesser rugby-playing nations.

"Danie scored a couple of tries and the guys had the bit between their teeth. The game was still ours, but yeah, the South African boys came back very well," recalls Strachan.

"It probably stood them in very good stead for the following few seasons that they could foot it with arguably one of the top sides in the world after being isolated for so long and show a bit of steel towards the end.

"It showed three years later when they won the World Cup. It was a good starting point for them."

Gerber also makes the point that South Africa had precious little time to prepare for their return match against the All Blacks.

"We didn't have much time to prepare and the odds were stacked against us," he recalls.

"The All Blacks hit us hard early, but things came together for us in the second half. The stadium was packed. It was a very emotional day.

"From a personal perspective I wanted the ball in my hands as soon as possible."

New Zealand hadn't enjoyed an ideal build-up.

"It was the last game of our tour and we had been in Australia for three or four weeks prior to coming out. The guys hadn't seen their families for close to two months. That was tough. Those things sometimes have an effect towards the latter stages of a game," says Strachan.

For the likes of Botha and Gerber, who were veterans of the controversial 1981 Springbok tour of New Zealand and who would probably have been acknowledged as greats on the world stage had South Africa's isolation not restricted them to sporadic appearances, this was a moment of huge significance.

"We were all growing up during the 1981 series against the Springboks. The guys that were still playing obviously had standing amongst us," says Strachan.

"I suppose the flip side was that Naas was also getting to the end of his career. There was a view that, while he was still a god in South Africa, the best part of his career was probably over. We looked at ways of exploiting that.

"Naas was pretty good in 1992, but he played his best football prior to that. It was a shame for Naas and Danie that they did not play much football between 1981 and their return. They wasted a large chunk of their international careers. They were world class.

"Danie was still on top of his game, but probably fell over pretty soon after that.

"Joost van der Westhuizen played for the Junior Springboks against us, so while some of those older guys were getting towards the end of their careers, there were a lot of talented young players coming through.

"They (the Junior Springboks) put up a really good fight at Loftus. I remember playing that game and Joost went on to become one of the best scrumhalves in the world. It was a bit of the old moving on and the new coming in."

Craven's warning about taking on the world's best teams too early proved to be an astute one. South Africa were thumped by Australia the following week and later that year under Williams' coaching they shared a series with France (they won 20-15 in Lyon and lost 16-29 in Paris) before being mauled 33-16 by England at Twickenham.

"Doc was right. He knew rugby," Luyt stated with hindsight. "We thought the Currie Cup made us the best rugby nation in the world. Springbok trials alone are 10 yards faster. I can only imagine what it must be like at international level."

There was much controversy in the aftermath, with events before and during the game showing that rugby unity was no more than an official agreement.

The Springbok team was unavoidably lily white – this would more often than not be the case until 1999 – and Luyt made the highly controversial and provocative decision to play the old South African anthem *Die Stem* before kick-off.

This was in spite of Sarfu reportedly having promised that the anthem would not be played.

It also wasn't as if the crowd was entering into the spirit of unity – a request for a moment of silence for peace and democracy was defied and old South African flags were waved all across the stadium.

South Africa, of course, was still some way off from democracy and there was neither a new flag to wave nor another anthem to sing.

But the South African flag of the time was considered a symbol of apartheid and the playing of the anthem was a clearly defiant act and hardly advocated inclusivity.

Luyt was unrepentant and believes the anthem helped galvanise the Springboks.

"It was the best anthem ever sung by 60-odd thousand people," he said.

"The fact is they were singing *Nkosi Sikelel' iAfrika* at soccer matches. There was no hard and fast rule. I discussed it with New Zealand Rugby Union chairman Eddie Tonks beforehand and he said 'by all means do it'. He denied it afterwards, of course.

"There were people who would have sung the anthem anyway come hell or high water.

"I have never seen such togetherness between people. I think it helped us in our effort against New Zealand. The players put on a hell of a show."

Politically incorrect as it was, the anthem antic did not necessarily go down badly with players. They simply wanted to play rugby and had no interest in the politics of the situation.

"It motivated us a great deal and we didn't even pay any attention to the political hullabaloo," recalls Gerber.

"We knew it would probably be the last time that we would be singing the anthem at such an event. There were thousands of old South African flags.

"Frankly I was just too happy to be able to play and pull the jersey over my head. I played in the old and new set-up, so nobody can take my blazer away!

"Just to play international rugby was great. It was special against the All Blacks because you knew you were playing against the best team in the world.

"It's such a pity we were hit by isolation. I would have liked to play 100 tests for South Africa. I was fed-up with the entire political situation. I was prepared to play with and against anybody."

The sentiment of just wanting to play rugby was probably a correct summary of the Springbok feeling rather than them being deliberately disrespectful. However, it pointed to naivety considering the political significance of the occasion. Luyt recalls having to appear in front of Sarfu's Executive Committee following the political fall-out from the anthem issue.

"The man who stood up for me was Doc Craven. He said, 'Gentlemen, let me tell you something, all I have heard from them (the politicians) has been 'us, us, us'. What about us? I felt proud on Saturday when we sang the anthem and of how the Springboks played. Let's think of us (ourselves) as well'.

"Craven was a wonderful man. We could not have political parties dictate to us. We had enough of that with the National Party."

But so incensed was the ANC that there was talk of the following Saturday's match against Australia being called off.

Joe French is reported to have played a big part in persuading the political party representing the majority of South Africans to allow it to go ahead.

As it happened, the Springboks got a reality check on just how far they had fallen behind as they were thumped 26-3 by the Wallabies at Newlands.

But what couldn't be denied amid all the controversy, agony and ecstasy is that South Africa was irreversibly on its way to democracy and the Springboks were back.

Springbok Backsides to the Wall

"The transformation from one weekend in which we got destroyed to the next and the points swing was so big that it was incredible."
— BRENDAN VENTER

If there is one thing that really irks the Springboks and their coaches, it's scathing criticism in the media by former players.

And Ian McIntosh's team got the royal treatment as they sat down for breakfast with Afrikaans daily newspaper *Die Burger* on the morning of 11 June 1994 – the day of the second test against England at Newlands.

Former Springbok flank Jan Boland Coetzee didn't mince his words, saying that the team captained by Francois Pienaar didn't deserve to be called Springboks. Rather, they should be called "Proteas".

"They give the impression that they don't want to play for their country. There is no pride among them. They are not physically up to it. They also don't have the discipline required of Springboks," Coetzee pontificated.

And, finally, his *coupe de grace*: "They are not worth a Springbok's backside."

Coetzee would have felt more than a little foolish when New Zealand referee Colin Hawke blew his final whistle shortly before 5pm after an inspired Springbok performance. South Africa had prevailed 27-9.

It was a spectacular turnaround after they had crashed to a 15-32 defeat in the first test at Loftus Versfeld just the previous Saturday.

Not many people saw the defeat at Loftus coming. And, in the wake of that unexpected setback, few anticipated the following weekend's resounding victory.

Prior to the debacle in Pretoria, the English had lost provincial encounters against Free State (11-22), Natal (6-21) and Transvaal (21-24). The latter defeat came just a week before the first test and England coach Dick Best had selected his strongest line-up. The outcome of that match possibly led to the Springboks underestimating the English and consequently paying a high price.

What happened at Loftus was considered much more than a defeat. It had been downright humiliating and was treated as a national disaster by the powers that be.

So much so that selection convenor Hannes Marais was told by Sarfu chairman Louis Luyt that they should postpone picking the team for the second test. They had planned to do so the very night that the Boks lost in Pretoria.

Luyt claimed he had got word from team manager Jannie Engelbrecht that the selectors were "too emotional" to pick a side and he wanted to bring in some outside help.

"Louis said we were a little 'confused' and wanted to arrange some assistance for us. He invited experts for a think tank and we convened at Ellis Park," Marais recalls.

The think tank was attended by McIntosh, the six selectors (Marais, assistant coach Gysie Pienaar, Willie Kahts, Dawie Snyman, Dougie Dyers and Jackie Abrahams), John Williams (Northern Transvaal), Nelie Smith (Free State), Kitch Christie, Ray Mordt (both Transvaal) and Ian Kirkpatrick (a former Springbok coach).

The discussions started at 10am and by 2pm the selectors could eventually get down to the business of picking a team.

"The selectors remained silent throughout the discussions and eventually Louis said that he had now heard everyone's opinion. He said 'Hannes, we've heard enough. You can now chair the selection committee again and pick a side'.

"I was really angry and told him that I hadn't been appointed as a convenor of 15 selectors. Louis was taken aback and I told them they could go and have lunch while we picked the team. He got very angry and said 'Listen here, I'll eat when I want to. Don't tell me when I must eat'."

The episode strained the relationship between the selectors and Sarfu management.

"We were furious that Louis had listened to Jannie's view that we were too emotional. No-one sat next to us at Loftus to see whether we were emotional or not. What happened was against Sarfu's regulations. But anyway . . ."

After all that, there were ultimately five changes and a positional switch from the team that lost the first test.

By far the most significant change was the selection of Johan Roux in place of Joost van der Westhuizen at scrumhalf. To many it will be unthinkable that the axing of Van der Westhuizen actually strengthened a side, but the selectors felt he had been too individualistic at Loftus. Roux was far less flashy, but could fit into a distinct pattern and be the battery in a team's watch.

The rest of the changes were all in the pack. Balie Swart moved across from tighthead to replace Ollie le Roux as the loosehead prop, with Johan le Roux handed the No 3 jersey.

Mark Andrews was also lined up for his first cap at lock with the intention that he should replace Steve Atherton. But an injury to Hannes Strydom meant that Atherton survived the culling and would partner Andrews.

The loose forward combination was reshuffled, with Adriaan Richter replacing Tiaan Strauss as No 8 and Ian Macdonald coming in for Fritz van Heerden on the flank.

Remarkably, the team that would take the field only had the total experience of 72 test caps between them. Of those, 39 were shared between right wing James Small, inside centre Pieter Müller and hooker John Allan. Nine of Allen's 13 caps had been in the colours of Scotland.

Roux, Andrews and Johan le Roux were all going to make their test debuts.

The Springbok starting line-up (with their test caps in parentheses) was as follows: André Joubert (4), James Small (13), Brendan Venter (1), Pieter Müller (13), Chester Williams (2), Hennie le Roux (3), Johan Roux (0), Adriaan Richter (3), Ian Macdonald (4), Francois Pienaar (8), Steve Atherton (3), Mark Andrews (0), Johan le Roux (0), John Allan (13), and Balie Swart (5).

They would be up against a vastly experienced England team and Marais admits that it was the one occasion where he had a sleepless night before a test.

But he found comfort on the morning of the game as he opened the Bible that the Gideons had placed in his hotel room.

"I read a Psalm that was very encouraging and when my wife woke up I told her that we were going to win the match. I had total peace," he says.

The game was a triumph for the Boks, with Roux's box kicks being the biggest thorn in England's flesh.

"I think the victory was partly down to very good coaching because Johan was picked ahead of Joost," recalls outside centre Brendan Venter.

"We decided that we were going to kick the leather off the ball. It was going to be wet at Newlands and we were going to smash them. Johan gave us a brilliant kicking game at scrumhalf and I just remember it must have been so hard to play against us. We were just unbelievably motivated because we had taken a lot of criticism that week.

"We just absolutely demolished England. The transformation from one weekend in which we got destroyed to the next and the points swing was so big that it was incredible."

South Africa could have won by a considerably bigger margin and, conversely, even flirted with disaster a little. Fullback André Joubert missed his first three penalties and England stayed in touch until deep into the second half.

But the breakthrough came a little over 10 minutes before full-time with a splendid try by Springbok flyhalf Hennie le Roux from a move off the base of the scrum.

Richter picked the ball up and broke wide before flicking it back to Pienaar. Le Roux timed his run perfectly and crashed his way through after taking the short pass from Pienaar. It's a try that will be considered a significant one in the annals of Springbok rugby for many years to come.

A try by Joubert followed as the Boks pushed home their advantage late in the game.

But the match could have been beyond England's reach much earlier as the Boks failed to convert many opportunities.

It matters little.

Roux's tactical nous and accurate execution with his kicking from the base brought the Springboks' marauding forwards into the game. They also dominated the set phases and were incisive on attack.

Significantly, it was South Africa's first test victory on home soil in the post-isolation phase. It was also a pleasing turnaround for Newlands as a venue as the previous test there had been the ignominious 3-26 defeat to Australia in 1992. Back then the Springboks had bitten off far more than they could chew on their immediate return to the international stage.

The match was the highlight of McIntosh's career as Springbok coach. He had succeeded John Williams in the hot seat and presided over a home series defeat to France, and series defeats in Australia and New Zealand.

It would be a superficial analysis to simply label his term a failure. South Africa were still feeling their way back into test rugby, but it did little to temper the expectations of the public.

Selection was a hot topic throughout McIntosh's tenure, with the coach at odds with Marais and other members of the committee over personnel and the playing style that should be followed.

McIntosh believed in so-called "direct rugby", which involved attacking the advantage line from flat-lying positions. The flyhalf and inside centre were key players in taking the ball up with the thinking that the ensuing phase play would create opportunities.

Marais' panel and a number of the players didn't believe in an approach that resulted in excessive collision in the inside channel and felt the predictability set the team on a road to nowhere.

As a result, McIntosh couldn't always select the players he wanted. He was very critical of Marais in his autobiography, even going as far as referring to the former Springbok captain as "someone from the distant past".

Marais, for his part, felt that McIntosh's rugby philosophy was shallow and wouldn't stand up to scrutiny against top opposition.

And, he says, he was not alone in his views.

"The entire selection committee disagreed with the way he wanted to play the game," says Marais.

"He absolutely insisted that we should pick players who would play his way, but the selection committee said 'no, we will pick the best players'.

"We were not going to pick players according to a set pattern. Rather, we would opt for players that had the potential and skill levels to play well at test level. That was our approach and it was nothing personal.

"We called Mac's way of playing 'crash ball'. We wanted players that could use their skill. It was just a matter of us wanting the team to play total rugby. We weren't prepared to omit more talented players because he wanted to play to a set pattern. He could not deal with or understand that.

"Perhaps we were unfair on him. But it was never personal from my side. It's just that we disagreed with him and wanted the team to play total rugby."

But Brendan Venter, who wore the No 13 jersey in both tests against England and has subsequently established himself as one of the foremost students of the game, believes circumstances at the time still dictated that teams approached matches without much of a game plan.

"We played poor rugby and weren't a good side," he says.

"You must remember that we got together on Mondays before tests. There were no moves, patterns, maps . . . nothing.

"Thinking about it now, it's a case of getting these unbelievably committed people who are prepared to die for their country and are going to go out there and try their best. But there isn't a plan. It's actually quite incredible.

"I look back at it all and realise the bit of a plan we had for the second test – kicking and chasing – was a lot more than we had in the first match. We had no plan for the first test. We'd do some backline moves in the build-up, a little bit of this and a little bit of that . . . I'm involved in coaching in the modern era and it's chalk and cheese."

While McIntosh's philosophy was a determining factor in the way the Boks played, Venter's statements are an affirmation that rugby was in the twilight of the amateur era. And there were a lot of factors outside of the coach's control.

And, says Venter, McIntosh didn't have a great crop of players at his disposal. As mentioned earlier, they were very inexperienced as South Africa had re-entered the international scene only two years previously.

The Newlands clash against England was only South Africa's 14th in the post-isolation phase.

"I believe that great coaches are made by great players, and with my hand on my heart, I don't think South Africa had a great crop of players in Mac's era.

I think that was because a lot of us were young and immature. We had just come back in 1992 and tried the likes of Naas Botha and Danie Gerber. Suddenly it was 1993 and we had to move on and build," says Venter.

"Poor Mac. Just go and look at how few test caps his teams had. Those players were a lot more mature when Kitch Christie (McIntosh's successor) got them. Suddenly Francois Pienaar had played more than 10 tests. The fact of the matter is that we just had a more mature side in 1995.

"It does beg the question: Is criticism of a coach really valid considering how little coaching there was in the old days. How much was it just a matter of the luck of getting a good team?"

As for McIntosh's philosophy, Venter believes it was "very good".

"His view is that if you get over the gain line, your whole team is behind the opponent's pack. So you have your 15 players against the opponent's seven backs.

"Mac pioneered the idea of getting over the gain line. Go and look at how successful he was as coach of Natal. If you look at all successful teams these days, they have a big inside centre who gets them over the gain line. It is a model that still works. These days they just add a lot more detail to it.

"Kitch could also select the core of the Transvaal team, who believed in him. Mac never had that privilege, so there wasn't a complete belief in him by the players. I think that was a big issue.

"It's essential that there is a good relationship between the coach and captain. You don't always get that at international level."

Le Roux also provides an important perspective on the conflicting views at the time.

"Mac had a very specific game plan and wanted it his way," Le Roux recalls.

"It possibly led to the perception that the Transvaal players weren't in tune with him. I played according to the game plan, but also felt that one should have freedom of choice on the field. But I can't say that any of the players were against Mac.

"His record at Natal speaks for itself and they were very successful playing that way. But Natal's loss to us (Transvaal) in the Currie Cup final in Durban (in 1993) was a result of predictability. We knew we had to protect the inside channel. The Sharks had the lion's share of possession, but there was a predictability about them even when there were opportunities out wide.

"I believe in structured play to break down defences, but there should always be variety. I didn't play under Mac for long. I think he felt that I didn't believe in his philosophy."

McIntosh, of course, had handed the Natal coaching reins over to Harry Viljoen by the time the 1993 Currie Cup final was played, but his philosophy on the game was still entrenched.

Transvaal had also won the Super10 series and were coached by Kitch Christie, who would succeed McIntosh as Springbok coach. Luyt's provincial affiliation was with Transvaal, which may have been a guiding factor in McIntosh's demise.

Marais found it easier to relate to Christie's coaching style.

"Kitch's coaching came from within the team and he didn't enforce a set pattern on the players. Mac's philosophy was too rigid. All you do is take the ball up and a ruck forms. If you have very strong forwards and good halfbacks, you can get away with it.

"But it's not good for the game and the players' development because you don't have to think. If you stop the attacking team and they get a slow ball from the ruck, they can't play.

"Mac always spoke of sucking in the defenders and when the ball came out your opponent would be outnumbered. But teams could opt to commit few players to the ruck. You just line up all your players on defence to stop that approach in its tracks.

"We didn't win the World Cup in 1995 with that. We enforced a superb defensive pattern and utilised the possession we got well."

Whatever the merits – or alleged lack – of the McIntosh-way, there can be little doubt that he did some important groundwork for Christie. Francois Pienaar was notably appointed captain.

And there can be even less doubt that McIntosh was on a hiding to nowhere. He had a meddling president in Luyt, an obstructive selection committee even if they felt they were acting in South African rugby's best interests and players who had their reservations about his playing philosophy.

Between Luyt, the selectors, McIntosh and the players there was a whole lot of infighting going on.

It was fertile ground for McIntosh's demise and it eventually came in the wake of South Africa's series defeat to the All Blacks in 1994. They could easily have won the series had they used their opportunities. It was a great chance missed as the Springboks had been up against a weak New Zealand side.

But 11 June 1994 at least was a day where everyone's plan appeared to come together at the same time.

McIntosh felt he finally did it his way, the selectors could reflect positively on the masterful choice of Roux at scrumhalf and there wasn't anything that Luyt would have felt required his immediate attention.

The joy would be short-lived, but abiding memories were nevertheless made. Le Roux's try will still be crystal clear in the memories of those who are old enough to recall it, and it completed a fitting passage of play for South Africa's first home test victory in the post-isolation phase.

The players had certainly distinguished themselves as being worth much more than a Springbok's backside.

CHAPTER 3

Divine Intervention?

"There were just too many coincidences. It defied the law of averages."
– BRENDAN VENTER

When referee Ed Morrison sounded the final whistle in South Africa's epic World Cup final victory over New Zealand on 24 June 1995, the first thing the Springboks did after jumping up in the air was to kneel down and pray.

Prayer is part of the South African rugby culture, in particular before games, where players from a young age bow their heads to thank their Lord for the opportunity and ask Him to keep them safe.

But this time it was to say thank you for what a number of them believed to be the culmination of a South African miracle.

Getting there had been a roller coaster ride with one twist of fate after the other.

Adversity had reared its head on a number of occasions but, even if the Springboks didn't know it themselves, they were an unstoppable force on their way to the 15-12 victory over the All Blacks.

To fully appreciate how a little bit of sporting history that tickled Hollywood's fancy was shaped, one can go back to the team the Springbok selectors named to play Western Samoa in a warm-up test prior to the tournament.

The team was what coach Kitch Christie considered South Africa's strongest available starting line-up and there was no sign of Joel Stransky, who would eventually emerge as South Africa's hero with the drop goal that clinched victory in the final.

Hennie le Roux was named at flyhalf, with Brendan Venter and Japie Mulder as the centre pairing.

However, Venter rolled an ankle in a match for Free State and was forced to withdraw on the Monday before the test. Consequently, Le Roux was moved to inside centre and Stransky was picked at flyhalf. It hadn't been intended to be that way.

South Africa thrashed the Samoans 60-8 but, as if to compound their woes, wing Chester Williams sustained a hamstring injury. Williams was still named in the World Cup squad, but eventually couldn't march on with the injury and was replaced by Pieter Hendriks.

It was another significant twist of fate as Hendriks produced one of the lasting images of the tournament by rounding the great but ageing Wallaby wing David Campese in the opening game against reigning champions Australia.

South Africa's magnificent 27-18 win over Australia set them on the high road to glory. Their fear of disappointing South African supporters was suddenly transformed into belief that they could go all the way. They were better than even they had thought.

Hendriks would play another two games against Romania and Canada before being suspended for his part in a brawl in the latter encounter.

By now Williams had fortunately recovered and he returned to score an impressive four tries in the 42-14 quarter-final victory over Western Samoa.

The semi-final against France in Durban was next and it was actually remarkable that the teams were even allowed to play on the waterlogged field, let alone that a late try that would have knocked South Africa out of the World Cup was disallowed.

Giant French flank Abdelatif Benazzi had pounced on a loose ball after an up-and-under and appeared to sail over the Bok line, but was adjudged by referee Derek Bevan to have been inches short. It was a call that would probably have been different had television match officials been used in those days.

It matters not. The Boks won 19-15 and were in the final.

If South Africa's semi-final victory over France in Durban was an unconvincing one, New Zealand's win over England in Cape Town was the polar opposite.

The Kiwis ruthlessly put the English to the sword, with devastating wing Jonah Lomu producing another of those lasting images as he bulldozed his way over England fullback Mike Catt in a 45-29 victory.

New Zealand were the overwhelming favourites for the final and the public's imagination had been gripped by the apparently unstoppable Lomu.

And for all the reverence of Christie – justified as it is for a man who went unbeaten through his tenure as Springbok coach – he had a plan for the final that his players didn't believe in.

Christie called the players into a room at the beginning of that week for a motivational talk that would also serve as the basis for his game plan.

The coach painted a picture of the Boks' superiority by highlighting their intellect and their academic qualifications compared to that of the All Blacks. It was a talk the team found most entertaining and motivating.

But their enthusiasm soon dissipated as Christie revealed his grand plan to beat the All Blacks: The Boks were going to speed the game up at every opportunity with tactics such as split kick-offs, tap penalties, short lineouts and quick throw-ins.

Split kick-offs would involve positioning forwards on both sides of the field, thereby making the Springboks' kick-off strategy unpredictable as opposed to conventional. But it would obviously give the All Blacks some space to attack.

This he called the "brains game" – an extension of his team talk – but the players feared it wasn't the cleverest thing to want to take the All Blacks on at their own strengths.

Christie had nevertheless shown himself unafraid to make bold decisions. He had omitted Tiaan Strauss from the World Cup squad out of concern that neither he nor Francois Pienaar would be willing to bow to the other.

He also made the controversial decision to pick lock Mark Andrews at No 8 at the expense of Rudolf Straeuli for the semi-final and final. It was a selection that horrified the press, but it accommodated Hannes Strydom in the team and the additional tall timber in the lineouts proved useful.

All players want is a plan, but here was one they didn't like and it took the gentle art of diplomacy to express their reservations.

Venter, a straight talker and never afraid to voice his opinion, was the first to get up and express his concern. But he was subtle enough.

"I think it's a really good idea, but maybe we shouldn't split the kick-offs because the All Blacks have devastating broken field runners and our strength lies in how tidy we are in the basics," he said.

A handful of the other deep thinkers in the squad also gave their input.

"I think it's a brilliant idea, but maybe we shouldn't take short lineouts because our lineout drive and pack has been really good. The moment we have short lineouts, we give the All Blacks broken field."

"I think it's a great idea, but maybe we shouldn't throw the ball in quickly at the lineouts. Why would we want to do that if our driving play from lineouts is our strength?"

And so forth . . .

But the "brains game" wasn't consigned to the recycle bin just yet. It would be trialled at the Boks' first training session in the build-up to the game. It proved a disaster.

The first tight forward to take a tap penalty on his 22-metre line was turned over and a try was conceded in the corner. As for the split kick-offs, they were a complete mess.

And so the brains game was downgraded to "Plan B" – read: on the scrap heap.

But who knows? If the Boks' execution had been better on the training field they may well have played a game with a high error-rate that the All Blacks would have fed off with Lomu, Walter Little, Frank Bunce, Jeff Wilson and Glen Osborne making up their backline from 11 to 15.

Naturally, Lomu occupied discussions and, according to Stransky, Christie had altered the defensive model slightly to push the All Blacks in-field.

"This would ensure that we maybe have a four on one against Lomu. We stood wider and had to make sure there were no gaps in midfield. We looked to James Small to get up quickly," recalls Stransky.

As it turned out, the pre-match hype about Lomu only served to motivate the Springboks. The one time that the giant wing cut the line, he was brought down with a brave front-on tackle from Bok scrumhalf Joost van der Westhuizen.

Mulder tackled him into touch on another occasion.

As for the game itself, Stransky and All Black flyhalf Andrew Mehrtens traded three-pointers in a typical low-risk affair.

South African flank Ruben Kruger also had a clear try ruled out in the first half.

We all know the rest and where we sat as it happened. Mehrtens fluffed his lines with an attempted drop goal that might have clinched the game towards the end of normal time and Stransky succeeded with his in extra time.

If we as supporters were nervous during the whole episode that stretched into extra time, the Boks were less so.

They had been in the proverbial zone as they made their way onto the field, with Christie and President Nelson Mandela having conjured up their powers of motivation without having to say much.

"We were very tense beforehand, but it all changed when Nelson Mandela walked into our dressing room and wished us good luck," Springbok hero Chester Williams recalls.

"It was almost as if to convey the message that he had taken the pressure onto his shoulders. When he walked out and the crowd went berserk, we realised what incredible support there was and that we had to win. We suddenly felt that the chance of us losing was very slim. Francois Pienaar (the Springbok captain) told us as much.

"We knew after 10 minutes into the game that we could win. Everyone thought New Zealand would beat us quite comfortably because they had hammered England and we didn't have as much talent as them. But I think we already won a psychological battle in facing their haka."

Kobus Wiese was the key man there as he moved in front of James Small, who would be Lomu's direct opponent. The giant lock stared Lomu down and the stage was set.

The debate early in the week had ultimately also yielded a game plan that rattled the All Blacks. It was based on the old adage that attack wins matches, but defence wins tournaments.

"With New Zealand having been so good against England, the general feeling was that there were a couple of guys we had to stop," recalls Venter.

"We had enormous belief in our defence, even though we very rarely practised it. It was just amazing how the guys defended. We actually ended up being the better team and created more opportunities.

"The outstanding thing for me was the composure both goalkickers showed on the day. Joel gets a lot of credit for that drop goal, but kicking the other 12 points under massive pressure was also exceptional."

So, is the aforementioned aimed at detracting from Christie? Not at all.

The fact that the intellectuals in the team were allowed to provide candid input actually highlighted one of the coach's strengths: his players were empowered to speak their minds.

He had also displayed the quality of any great coach by not being afraid to make big calls and stick to them. The appointment of Pienaar as captain was obviously crucial in fostering a remarkable unity and sense of purpose in the team. And, of course, he picked Andrews at No 8.

Then there were his immense powers of motivation. All he had to tell the Springboks prior to the final, when he detected their focus, was that he felt "sorry for New Zealand" as he wouldn't want to play against them. And, of course, he had picked powerful personalities without feeling threatened. But rugby is a game of variables, which is why one often hears coaches and players speak of "the bounce of the ball" or "fifty-fifty decisions" not going their way.

It basically comes down to a player being lauded for a great try when he himself didn't play any role in beating the fullback. If the ball bounces awkwardly for the defender and you happen to score, it's just pot luck.

Similarly, the appointment of a referee is a variable no team can control. The approach to the issue by virtue of adaptive and constructive engagement is.

A classic example was the "try" by Kruger in the final that wasn't awarded. Nothing the Springboks did could change the decision, so the discipline was to show the mental strength to deal with it and retain their resolve.

And that is where the old chestnut of "making your own luck" applies.

But Venter, who is as logical a man as you can get, reckons the way in which everything fell into place for the Springboks in 1995 was just simply too good to be true.

"We went down on our knees afterwards and Francois just thanked

God for the opportunity of being involved in the final. I often look back at the whole thing and think that maybe we were less involved than we thought," he says.

"Imagine if I hadn't been injured and Joel never played. Then there was Chester's return after Pieter Hendriks was suspended and it just about bound the nation together. Suddenly there was this one big star and he was a black guy. Chester scored four tries against Samoa and suddenly the belief came flooding.

"There were so many little things that went our way within that entire process. Go and look at Benazzi's 'try'. If that was replayed, you would probably have seen from all angles that he had scored. I think he scored. He was lying on the ball and everyone was around him. But the referee couldn't award the try because he couldn't see it.

"You look back at those things and you always want to reflect on your personal contribution. But ultimately these wonderful games are built around so many things that go right. And we are not as in control of them as we think."

Does he think God's hand was in it?

"Yes. You look back and see how many things just went in our favour. I believe there is a God and that is my only take on the thing. I can't see it differently. There were just too many coincidences. It defied the laws of averages.

"There is a certain humility involved in the process. You know that you have worked hard and achieved something, but even the people who aren't believers will look at it and think something else happened."

But why would God want South Africa to win?

"That part I don't know because I'm a simple human being. I don't know God's mind. It's a good question, but it's the whole issue here. I don't pray to win because I don't understand the bigger picture.

"All I know is that the recipe for success is not as simple as doing

46

something and getting the outcome you want. There are factors outside of our control."

While some may scoff at it, a spiritual take on the event is not out of place considering a few of the myths.

One of those was the involvement of Mandela, whose role, inasfar as the team was concerned, was to visit and use his considerable charisma to help motivate them.

Notwithstanding the immortal images and their underlying symbolism, the notion that he had worked with a "grand plan" as depicted in the movie *Invictus* is questionable.

"It wasn't a case of Mandela manipulating everything. I don't think he's that kind of person," says Venter.

"The nice thing about meeting him was that I felt in my heart that here was a genuine person. When I looked at him I saw joy in his eyes. It felt as if he cared for the cause as much as if he was a supporter.

"That is how I experienced him. Not that he was busy with this massive political plan.

"I could not reconcile the person I met with what I read of him before he was imprisoned. My respect for Mandela was born out of that. How could a person with so much anger after being jailed for so long have so much forgiveness and be unconditionally kind to other people? That was incredible."

Stransky's match-winning drop goal also fell into the incredible category. It highlighted the Springboks' mental strength and accuracy of execution on the day.

"We had called a back-row move but, as Joost van der Westhuizen fed the ball into the scrum, I saw that the way the All Blacks had lined up left a huge channel for a drop goal. I called it to Joost and he cancelled the blind side move we had planned. The drop was a great strike. I hit it sweetly and it would never deviate," the flyhalf recalls.

It was a moment that highlighted another truth that is often overlooked: a coach is only as good as his players.

Had the Springboks capitulated in the face of the might of the All Blacks, Christie would have faced a barrage of criticism. There would doubtless have been reflections on it being a massive error of judgement to leave Strauss out and to play Andrews at No 8.

But it's those small margins that shape our reality and truth. And, of course, give rise to our myths.

To this day, the class of 1995 is a remarkably humble bunch. The vast majority of them are successful people and do not dine out on their past glories.

Not all of them share the same religious convictions, but all were humbled by being part of a remarkable episode in South Africa's history.

If God did indeed intervene, He may have done so on the basis that South Africa was a country on the edge. The Rainbow Nation needed something to unify its people and it came packaged in the Rugby World Cup.

Whatever the case, we will pobably never see a rugby match of such significance as the World Cup final of 1995.

It was a moment where an entire country held hands. Divine intervention or not, it was a defining moment in the modern history of rugby union and indeed in the history of South Africa.

Out of Sight, Out of Mind

*"Nelson Mandela whispered into my ear just before the final to say that
he was very proud of me and that I should continue doing what I did before.
He said that the world was watching me."*
— CHESTER WILLIAMS

It is one of those strange coincidences that matches against Samoa played an important part in the Springboks' triumphant World Cup campaigns of 1995 and 2007.

And, in each instance, it was their left wing that scored a remarkable four tries – Chester Williams in 1995 and Bryan Habana in 2007.

Habana's feat in the 59-7 victory at the Parc des Princes in Paris would catapult him into the realm of super-stardom as he finished the tournament with eight tries. He was later crowned as the International Rugby Board's Player of the Year.

But it's doubtful whether an individual Springbok performance has carried as much meaning – or ever will – as the one by Williams in the 42-14 win over Western Samoa at Ellis Park in Johannesburg on 10 June 1995.

Without that victory – and with the only non-white player in the starring role – the scenes of jubilation that followed the World Cup final victory over the All Blacks might not have featured so many black faces.

And what adds to the feel-good factor is that it all happened on a stroke of good fortune.

Williams had earlier withdrawn from the World Cup squad after struggling with a hamstring injury and was replaced by Pieter Hendriks ahead of South Africa's opening match against Australia at Newlands.

Hendriks would memorably round ageing Wallaby wing David Campese in the 27-18 victory, but in a significant twist of fate he would be suspended for his role in a brawl in the match against Canada in Port Elizabeth.

That paved the way for Williams's re-entry after he had previously been resigned to setting his sights on playing in the 1999 World Cup.

But his return meant that South Africa had re-gained the talented man on whom the nation-building potential of the tournament had partly hinged.

"My face had been up everywhere on posters and there was a lot of hype about me. I was aware of my role and the public had high expectations. Then I got injured," Williams recalls.

"That's just how it goes in sport. It was a big disappointment for me and my teammates. Kitch Christie (coach) and Morné du Plessis (team manager) wanted me to play even if it would only be for a few minutes, but I could not let my country down."

"As a non-white person, me being there was very relevant on a personal and team level. It was very important that I be there so that the world could see that everyone had equal opportunities.

"When I got injured it was a bit of a political issue. But the history books reflect that I came back and that we won the World Cup.

"I still think Pieter was a hero because the try he scored was an important one and he rounded one of the best wings in the world to score in a game against the reigning champions. He played his part in getting us to the final, but I grabbed my opportunity when it presented itself."

And how.

Williams's four tries were all scored on the far left of the field – two either side of half-time – and highlighted his exceptional finishing ability.

Fullback André Joubert was the provider for the first as he found Williams on his left, while the winger finished in the same corner after good linking play with hooker Chris Rossouw and flank Ruben Kruger for the second.

The third again highlighted the late Kruger's immense contribution to the Springbok cause as he ran a clever line to beat the first line of defence and then defied heavy traffic to pass over the defence to his left. The ball travelled down to Williams and he scored another try in the corner.

Williams then became the first Springbok to score four tries in a test with one he reckons should perhaps not have been awarded. Scrumhalf Joost van der Westhuizen tapped and Williams came in to cover scrum-half after the ruck had formed.

The Boks' left wing then caught the Samoans napping on the right-hand side of the ruck and dived over, but he reckons he may not have grounded the ball in the act of "scoring". It matters little.

"The game against Samoa was a very emotional one for me because of my return to the side from injury," says Williams.

"There was a lot of pressure on me. People really wanted me to do well. My job was to score tries in whichever way and I don't think I disappointed. It was special to do that in the World Cup.

"The politics didn't bother me. I knew why I was there and believed I was the best in my position. All I had to do was to go out and show why I was picked."

As time passed before and during the tournament, the Springboks also warmed to the bigger picture in South Africa and it fuelled their desire.

"I don't think all the guys understood the bigger picture to begin with," says Williams.

"But Doc Louis Luyt (the then president of Sarfu) started interacting more with Nelson Mandela (then the president of South Africa) and Morné du Plessis.

"I think it's then that the players realised the significance of the World Cup for South Africa.

"Nelson Mandela spoke to us and explained why it was important. Some of the players wondered why we had to hold coaching clinics in Khayelitsha and Soweto, but he explained the importance of it to us.

"When we got there and little boys called us by name, the guys realised that those kids were following them and grasped what it was all about."

Williams would also forge a close relationship with Mandela – during and after the tournament.

"He spoke to me a little more than the others because I think he realised that I was under a lot of pressure with the weight of expectation. It was not so much a case of me having to prove myself. It was just that there would be broader support for the Springboks if I did well as a player of colour," says Williams.

"Apart from being significant to our team and country, it was also for Madiba. He used the Springbok team to be a more successful president.

"He whispered into my ear just before the final to say that he was very proud of me and that I should continue doing what I did before.

"We got to know one another well. I often went for meals at his residence and took my family along on a few occasions. He was very eager to meet the children and we are very fortunate to have had that interaction.

"Everyone says he is an amazing man, but you will only truly grasp the fact when you have seen him up close. He just has a remarkable presence about him."

Indeed, Madiba Magic runs like a golden thread through Springbok rugby.

But whether Mandela was working with such an expansive grand plan as was sketched in John Carlin's *Playing With The Enemy* – the book on which the film *Invictus* was based – is doubtful.

Williams nevertheless said that *Invictus* was mostly accurate in its depiction of the event and was even an eye-opener to some of the squad. He specifically mentioned Mandela calling Springbok captain Francois Pienaar to a meeting before the tournament.

"There are a lot of things that happen behind the scenes that players are not aware of. It was an eye-opener when we saw the movie. I'm talking about the political aspect. There are things that are hidden from the players so that they don't get intimidated," says Williams.

"For example, we didn't even know that Francois had been called in. They wanted to keep that quiet. It's just the way it works."

Williams also cites Luyt, who passed away in February 2013, as a key figure. Sarfu's president of the time was a much maligned leader and everything but a diplomat, but came packaged with savvy and had his hands on the team and tournament.

"Doc Luyt became such a successful person because he knew exactly what went on in politics, sport and business. He understood the interaction," says Williams.

In fact, Williams believes that the Boks' semi-final against France may well have been called off had it not been for Luyt. The field was water-logged and the French would have advanced to the final by virtue of a superior disciplinary record if the match wasn't played.

"We were told to warm up on four occasions. Doc Luyt was pacing around in his green blazer and saying 'Don't worry, we are going to play'. He knew that it would be curtains for us if we didn't play and saw to it that the field was in playable condition, even if it was still very wet."

He also believes Luyt took a necessary step to effect a coaching change after the Springboks had returned a beaten bunch from New Zealand under the guidance of Ian McIntosh.

"The appointment of Kitch was crucial because he brought a new dimension to our playing style and mindset. I think Doc Luyt forced it on South African rugby," says Williams.

"Mac perhaps overdid the gainline-driven game. There wasn't varia-tion and the top countries can match you because they also have big and strong players. What then?"

Williams likens the late Christie to the great former Manchester United football manager Sir Alex Ferguson.

"Kitch managed the team well and was prepared to get input from senior players. He worked according to the team's strengths and you couldn't move him on a point if he knew that he was right. But he took full responsibility if the team followed the instruction and it didn't work out. Most of what he did worked in any event," recalls Williams.

"There was good communication and we could go and speak to him at any time. He was way before his time. He was a disciplinarian, but with a human touch. He would let something be, but go and think it over and then call you in or just say something in passing. It's then that you real-ised what he was trying to get across.

"And, of course, he was fanatical about fitness. I think he realised we weren't the most talented team in terms of skill, but knew we had enough talent to get to the required level through hard work and being a super-fit team. He picked the players accordingly."

Apart from Pienaar's great leadership, Williams highlights the excep-tional contribution of flyhalf Joel Stransky over and above the drop goal that won the final.

"Joel is the guy I believe should really get a lot of credit for the team. Francois was the captain, so obviously there would have been a greater focus on him. But I think Joel played a big part in our success. He scored a try in the opening game against Australia, made a big contribution with his kicking and was a strong leader within the team."

Personality, in fact, was written all over the Springbok team and Williams' entry against Western Samoa added yet another man with the mental steel needed for the big occasion.

"Every guy from 1 to 15 was mentally very strong. Sizing up a player's leadership abilities is an important part of selection. That's where we were particularly strong in 1995 and the same applied to the team that won the World Cup in 2007," says Williams.

"Initially there may not be cohesion and you have to get to know one another. You have different cultures – Afrikaans, English, I'm a coloured . . . that's where you measure a coach. He knows what needs to be done technically, but how do you marry different personalities and make it a successful team, specifically in a country like South Africa?"

Christie was able to tap into that and the result was there for all to see. The team's unity and resolve took them all the way.

Williams recalls the joyful scenes immediately after the final and the street where his parents live was flooded with people celebrating.

"We were about an hour late for the post-match function because the bus couldn't get away. Everyone wanted to touch us. You just see people and skin colour is forgotten.

"I phoned home to my parents and the street in front of their house in Paarl was closed off. A huge number of people had pitched at their home. My dad said he just let them all in and they could do what they want. There was no way of stopping them because there were so many people and they were all celebrating."

There were remarkable scenes of unity between black and white in a country once deeply divided, but as one of its architects Williams feels it was all too brief.

"It was great to see that we could all share the joy and live together in harmony. It's just a pity that we didn't build on that. I'm referring to our politics and society. We ultimately didn't embrace it. We need a united country," he says.

It was fitting that Williams would play such a pivotal role.

He was the first player of colour to play test rugby for South Africa after unity was achieved, making his debut in the 52-23 win over Argentina in Buenos Aires on 13 November 1993.

While the match against Western Samoa highlighted Williams's exceptional finishing ability, a standout feature of his game was his work-rate. He was a left wing, but one often saw him pop up on the right.

"I didn't have the blistering pace of a David Campese and had to adapt my style accordingly. Rather than wait for the ball to come my way, I went to look for work and tried to get involved," he says.

"It was very enjoyable. I wanted people to see that I was more than just a wing with try-scoring ability. I often sat at home studying videos and in a way coached myself. The one thing I had to work very hard on was taking the high ball. I struggled at first, but in the end I mastered the skill."

Williams was only 24 during South Africa's World Cup campaign, but his career was interrupted by injuries.

He played nine tests in his final season of international rugby, with his swansong coming as a substitute in the 23-13 win over Wales in Cardiff on 26 November 2000.

By then former Springbok coach Harry Viljoen had already floated the idea of Williams joining his management as assistant coach after the tour.

But there was still life in Williams' 30-year-old legs and he continued to soldier on for the Cats before realising on their Australasian tour of 2001 that he had fallen out of love with the game.

"I went to Laurie Mains [the then Cats coach] while we were on tour and told him I didn't think I wanted to play anymore. He said I should continue, but I responded that I couldn't give him what he wanted. He said that I should go home and think it over. I didn't change my mind," he recalls.

"I think I could have played on, but I felt tired. I had struggled with injuries in 1996 and 1997 after tearing knee ligaments and by 1998 I felt

I had to constantly battle hard to get into the team. I wasn't involved in the World Cup in 1999 and there wasn't another one to look forward to at that stage of my career, so I decided to retire.

"I'm glad I did because I was able to end my playing career on my terms. No-one told me that I should retire and it wasn't the result of not being picked. They were still keen to pick me, but I didn't want to be picked."

Williams nevertheless told Sarfu that he wanted to stay involved in the game and they responded by adding him to the management of the national sevens team. He then took over as coach from Norman Mbiko at the end of a disappointing campaign in the World Sevens Series in 2001.

His coaching career has subsequently been something of a roller coaster ride and at the time of writing he found himself in obscurity in Romania.

There, in the western city of Timisoara, the man fondly remembered – but apparently almost forgotten – as the *Black Pearl*, was holding out hope but was not overly optimistic about a return to South Africa's rugby structures.

He was in his second season of coaching Timisoara, with whom he had won the Romanian championship the previous season.

It was also his second coaching spell in Romania after earlier achieving success in charge of Dinamo. Williams's rugby footprint since 2006 had also covered Uganda and Tunisia.

The irony of it is immense when one considers that, during his spell as South Africa's national sevens coach in 2002 and 2003, it was considered only a matter of time before he would coach the Springbok 15-man side.

But so big was the fallout in the wake of South Africa's disastrous World Cup campaign in 2003 that the governing body's leadership was overhauled. Rian Oberholzer left as chief executive of Sarfu and Silas Nkanunu was ousted as president by Brian van Rooyen.

Williams was no longer considered a Springbok coach in waiting and took a wrong turn on his coaching journey when he left the sevens team for a caretaker role at the Cats in Super Rugby after Tim Lane had been dismissed midway through the 2004 campaign.

The 2005 season proved a disappointment under Williams and the rug was pulled from underneath him at a time that he felt he was on the verge of finding his feet in the demanding job of coaching a team that was an uncomfortable marriage of the Lions and Free State.

He also had to put up with his wife being stalked during a spell at the Pumas and he would later get involved in a coaching job that constituted no more than crisis-management at Boland.

Williams's subsequent path has amounted to a disappearing act – a remarkable case of out of sight and out of mind. And an inappropriate one when his role in the shaping of South African rugby is considered.

His story is perhaps one that South African rugby has not drawn enough latter day inspiration from.

Its relevance will certainly never date and it is doubtful whether any rugby player in future will ever play a more meaningful role in South African society.

CHAPTER 5

Allez Les Boks!

"There was no way that I was going to play 10-man rugby.
South African players have skill and pace. We must never deny
ourselves the opportunity of using it."

– NICK MALLETT

"It was French rugby played against France."

That phrase, spoken by a French official to Springbok coach Nick Mallett, was probably the best way to describe South Africa's 52-10 victory over Les Bleus at the Parc des Princes on 22 November 1997.

The match will always be remembered for the remarkable individual performance by left wing Pieter Rossouw, who scored four of South Africa's seven tries.

But Rossouw was quite right in thanking his team-mates straight after the match. It was a fabulous team performance, with the final try by Henry Honiball capturing everything that was good about it as the ball travelled through numerous Springbok hands before the flyhalf dummied and scored.

So impressive were South Africa that they briefly turned the knowledgeable crowd into Springbok supporters. France were jeered off the field and South Africa was cheered on a lap of honour after the final whistle.

South Africa had managed a narrow 36-32 win over the French in Lyon the previous week. The Boks had built a commanding 36-15 lead, but ultimately had to survive a few anxious moments as the French scored three tries in a face-saving last quarter.

"I think the guys couldn't believe that we were leading by that much

59

and then they came back to 36-32. So it was quite tense in the end. What we learned from that was that you don't just give France the ball. You have to keep playing with it," Mallett recalls.

And so the Boks did the following week. So impressively, in fact, that it challenges one's perceptions of the so-called traditional South African strengths, which are based on physicality.

The Springboks are generally not expected to put teams to the sword as flamboyantly as the All Blacks. But this performance – and possibly South Africa's approach for the whole of 1997 - turned all that on its head as they kicked off from a 28-3 half-time lead and sustained the effort over the full 80 minutes.

"I remember saying to the guys in the change room [at half-time] that we have a unique opportunity to break world records here," Mallett says.

"I told them this is the most demoralised French side I've ever seen. The crowd was booing them and the guys didn't want to be on the field. They had completely given up. If we just continued to be positive and have a go, we could put them to the sword. We really did.

"We just kept the ball and broke their line with ease. We scored from lineouts, scrums, counter-attacks . . .. It was an outstanding attacking performance.

"What we did that day is what the All Blacks often do to the opposition. The French were cowering from our onslaught. They just didn't think that they could compete with us – physically, technically or from a skills point of view.

"I spoke to Fabien Galthie, who played in that game, and he said after 20 minutes there wasn't a single Frenchman talking on the field. There were two crying in the change room at half-time. It was a completely broken team. We played France into a situation where they didn't know what to do with the ball."

Mallett also felt that the talent at his disposal would be wasted on a game plan that inhibited their attacking strengths.

"I knew that Henry Honiball had the ability to get a backline going because he took the ball to the line. He was a threat. Joost van der Westhuizen was also a threat at scrumhalf and I had a very good passing centre in Dick Muir. He had huge confidence and a real belief in holding onto the ball. André Snyman was also a great runner . . . big and fast.

"And then there was a great back three. I put Percy Montgomery at fullback and Pieter Rossouw on the left wing. I had James Small on the right wing for the first tour and then Stefan Terblanche, who scored heaps of tries.

"That backline was a very skilful and physical one. I also had loose forwards who could complement it. Rassie Erasmus and Gary Teichmann both played linking games. Gary used to off-load a lot and never went to ground. He had the ability to pass in the tackle.

"Then you had André Venter, who could take the ball over the advantage line. Mark Andrews, Adrian Garvey and James Dalton could also run with the ball. Os du Randt had great hands.

"There was no way that I was going to play 10-man rugby. South African players have skill and pace. We must never deny ourselves the opportunity of using it."

That bold approach was handsomely rewarded at the Parc des Princes, but not before the Boks had to do their fair share of defending.

Having started the match splendidly with Snyman's try after just two minutes – it had its origin in a counter-attack launched by the irrepressible Montgomery – the Boks found themselves under the cosh for over 10 minutes.

However, the flow of the game was irreversibly changed when Erasmus intercepted a pass by French hooker Marc del Maso intended for lock Olivier Brouzet on the Bok 22.

Erasmus raced all the way through to the French 22-metre area and found Rossouw with a pass to his inside just as he was about to be hauled in. Honiball added the extras and the Boks were up 14-3.

The lead was extended when Teichmann was driven over under the posts. Rossouw closed out the half with his second try. It all started with clean possession from a scrum. The ball was then taken through two phases before Venter broke the line. He found Montgomery, who then floated the ball out to Small. The right wing cut back inside and gave the final pass to Rossouw back on the outside.

It was a well-deserved reward for Rossouw's appetite for work, which saw him pop up on the opposite wing. Honiball's fourth conversion made the score 28-3 and Mallett was determined that his side should not take their feet off the French players' throats.

The players heeded their coach's words.

Rossouw brought up his hat-trick shortly after the restart, with the Boks opting to spread the ball from a scrum in their own half. The set-piece had been won thanks to a tremendous tackle by Du Randt on French full-back Jean-Luc Sadourny, with the giant loosehead prop driving his man back in the tackle.

South Africa highlighted their attacking prowess by scoring the try off first phase.

Muir found Montgomery with a skip pass and he in turn passed to Rossouw, who beat his man with a subtle step inside and then raced away from the French defence before finally beating Sadourny. Honiball increased the lead to 35-3 with his conversion.

But Rossouw's *coup de grace* was yet to come.

This time the lineout was used as a launch pad, with Andrews taking Dalton's throw. The ball went down the line, with Honiball and Muir combining for a runaround before the flyhalf fed Rossouw.

Rossouw attacked the space and beat the defence on his inside and outside before breaking inside twice and spinning out of the tackle of French No 8 Abdelatif Benazzi.

The score increased to 42-3 and the French had been reduced to a rabble.

Hooker Rafael Ibanez scored France's only try after the Boks had added a penalty, but the scoring was completed by a remarkable team try which was finished by Honiball.

It was a fitting way to round off the scoring in a performance worthy of every superlative in the rugby lexicon.

Rossouw would turn into something of an enigma in South African rugby as he mixed the sublime with the ridiculous. What was never in doubt was his genius. It was the product of both abundant natural talent and a studious approach which would later see him leave his mark on backline coaching.

There was a flaky element about Rossouw as well and he sometimes left supporters' hearts in their mouths.

It wasn't something that ever concerned Mallett.

"Pieter had a lot of confidence in himself. He was one of the earliest wingers to understand the value of going for the intercept. He could spot very early whether the opposition would play it flat or whether they would opt for a wide pass. And woe betide a team that floated a wide pass with Pieter there.

"He was 1,93m tall and had these long arms. Shit, he would get his hands on anything. He picked out lots of interceptions and just sniffed out tries. He was defensively sound and very good under the high ball. Pieter was a very under-rated player."

Rossouw had already impressed when Mallett's predecessor, Carel du Plessis, picked him during the turbulent series against the British and Irish Lions earlier that year.

The second test on tour against France was his ninth in the Green and

Gold and he was emerging as a serious force in a game plan that was quite ironically built at the modest Boland Stadium in Wellington.

It was as coach of the Boland Cavaliers in 1997 that Mallett developed one of the Boks' party tricks under his coaching: opting to kick for touch and set up the lineout rather than going for the posts.

"Funnily enough, I used most of those moves (on tour) at Boland. When I met with the team before the tour, I asked them what they would like to keep from what they had been doing as they had beaten Australia 61-22 in their last game. Gary and the guys said that they would like to start afresh.

"We had 10 days in Johannesburg before we left, so I sat down and wrote out all my attacking moves with Boland. We taught them that in a week.

"I then said to the blokes that we are going to do things differently than before. We were not going to kick at poles that often. I believed we were much better than the teams we were playing against and we would try to multiply our try-scoring opportunities. So we were going to try and go for 5 points and hopefully 7.

"We scored lots of tries from lineout drives and also had backline moves involving blindside wingers. That is why Pieter scored so many tries in that game [against France]."

Teichmann's try was a direct result of the bold approach of opting for a kick to touch. The Boks were awarded a penalty just outside the French 22-metre area and it would be simple for Honiball to just stroke it over for the three points.

Instead, the Boks set up the lineout and after two phases Teichmann was driven over under France's posts. As a consequence the Boks led 21-3 rather than 17-3.

It's an approach that had the obvious potential to backfire and would inevitably be judged on the outcome alone.

64

South Africa's captain, Francois Pienaar, salutes the crowd from Hennie le Roux's shoulders after the 15-12 victory over New Zealand in the World Cup Final at Ellis Park in 1995.

Above: Louis Luyt *(Photograph by Leon Botha,* Beeld)

Top: The Springboks line up for the anthems before kick-off in their first match back from isolation against New Zealand at Ellis Park in 1992.

Right: Hennie le Roux celebrates after his brilliant try in South Africa's 27-9 victory over England at Newlands in 1994.

Bottom: Chester Williams and Jonah Lomu were central figures during the 1995 World Cup for different reasons. Lomu scored eight tries for the All Blacks in the tournament, while Williams played a key role in uniting his country. South Africa's 'Black Pearl' scored four tries in their 42-14 quarter-final victory over Samoa.

Above: The ultimate statesman, Nelson Mandela, works his charm at the 1995 World Cup.

Above: The Springboks kneel down to pray after their victory in the 1995 final.

Top left: Francois Pienaar and 1995 World Cup-winning coach, Kitch Christie, share a moment during training.

Top right: Getting a rain-soaked field in playing condition was a massive challenge before the World Cup semi-final against France in Durban in 1995.

Above: The outrageously-gifted Bob Skinstad works his magic with the ball in hand.

Top: Pieter Rossouw scores the try that secured South Africa's 13-3 victory over New Zealand at Athletic Park in Wellington in 1998. It was the Springboks' first victory over the All Blacks in New Zealand since 1981.

Above: Jannie de Beer kicks one of his famous drop goals in the quarter-final against England at the Stade de France in Paris, in 1999.

Top: Nick Mallett, assistant coach Alan Solomons and Brendan Venter look on as the Springboks set about their business during the 1999 World Cup. Venter provided Mallett with the blueprint for their 44-21 quarter-final victory over England, in which Jannie de Beer slotted a world record five drop goals.

Above: Robbie Fleck on his way to the tryline during a superb individual display in the 46-40 victory over the All Blacks at Ellis Park in 2000.

Left: Marius Joubert celebrates during the 40-26 victory over the All Blacks at Ellis Park in 2004. Joubert became only the second Springbok to score three tries in a test against New Zealand, following in the footsteps of Ray Mordt.

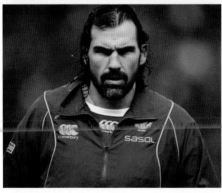

Above: Victor Matfield

Right: South African fans held Schalk
Burger in particularly high regard.

Top: The South African triumvirate of (from the left) captain John Smit,
coach Jake White and star player Schalk Burger with the spoils after the
International Rugby Board's annual awards ceremony in 2004. South
Africa was named the team of the year, while White and Burger were
respectively crowned Coach and Player of the Year.

Mallett's Springboks were hardly a conventional lot and were writing their own blueprint. They left the Northern Hemisphere having scored a staggering 35 tries in five tests (nine against Italy, 12 in two tests against France, four against England and 10 against Scotland.

Their coach's personality was as much of a catalyst as their talent.

"That team had a real belief that we could score tries and also believed in the way we were playing. Not only did each individual become very confident in his ability, but they were given carte blanche to have a crack and were good enough to do it. It's fantastic when that happens," says Mallett.

"I was also incredibly confident as a coach and absolutely convinced that we were better than our opponents. A number of players said that it showed and infused them with confidence.

"There weren't any negative thoughts that we couldn't do this or couldn't do that. If the opponents weren't 10 yards back, we had to have a crack. The approach wasn't disorganised. In fact, it was really well organised. But within that organisation the team had the freedom to play."

Mallett could comfortably afford to empower his players. There was a tremendous attacking threat among his backs, he had skilful loose forwards and the pack was physical and skilful in equal amounts.

An analysis of the tries that the Boks scored also suggested that the pioneering approach was the right one.

"I did an analysis of the tour in 1997 and found that over 40% of our tries stemmed from going for the corner instead of the poles. No one had done that before at international level," says Mallett.

"We kept it up in 1998. It can be rewarding when you have a team like New Zealand under pressure with a good pack of forwards at your disposal. You don't often get them within 10 metres of their try-line.

"If you only attack from scrum ball in the opposition's 22-metre area or from lineout ball from the 10-yard line down, you will have opportunities. But it won't be as many as when you get to within five metres of the line with a kick.

"In fact, the law was changed to the lineout having to be at least five metres away from the try-line as a result of what we did. We kicked it a yard out and then you could throw it to Mark Andrews. You could just drive over for the try and it was game over."

A number of records were equalled or broken in the victory against France.

As far as the points margin was concerned, it was South Africa's biggest over France, surpassing the 38-5 win of 1913 in Bordeaux. On top of that, it was the first time in France's history that they conceded more than 50 points in a test.

Rossouw also became the second only Springbok after Chester Williams to score four tries in a test. Williams had achieved the feat in South Africa's 42-14 win over Western Samoa in the 1995 World Cup tournament.

South Africa would continue to break records on their tour, including the 29-11 victory over England at Twickenham and a 68-10 slaughter of Scotland at Murrayfield.

Rossouw believes there were a number of factors that brought about the Springboks' radical transformation after all the trauma earlier in the year.

"Nick was a very charismatic person and a strong leader, which obviously played a role," he says.

"We also did some new things on that tour. Western Province were very strong that year under the coaching of Harry Viljoen, who got some of his ideas from Rod Macqueen [the former Wallaby coach].

"Alan Solomons, who was the Springbok backline coach, had worked with Harry at Western Province. That obviously helped Nick and he picked a large contingent of Western Province and Free State players after they played in the Currie Cup final. The guys were happy with Nick and there was a very good vibe in the team."

An understated component of the team that beat France in Paris, was the forced selection of Werner Swanepoel at scrumhalf after Joost van der Westhuizen was injured. Van der Westhuizen will no doubt go down as one of, if not the, greatest scrumhalves to wear South Africa's No 9 jersey, but Swanepoel came packaged with his own strengths.

The chief among those was quick passing from the base, which gave a brilliant backline more space. Van der Westhuizen had been injured in the first test against France, while an injury to fullback Justin Swart in the first test of the tour against Italy allowed Percy Montgomery to make the No 15 jersey his own.

Montgomery had made his debut with Rossouw as an outside centre in the second test against the British and Irish Lions earlier that year. He played six tests in the No 13 jersey and in spite of his attacking brilliance was exposed on defence – particularly by All Black No 13 Frank Bunce.

The centre combination of Muir and Snyman also worked for the Boks. Muir had a terrific passing game, while Snyman used his pace particularly well. He had been picked as a wing earlier that year and Mallett did well to restore him to his natural position.

Snyman left an indelible mark on the tour with a superb try against England at Twickenham and it's a pity that he increasingly relied on physicality in the ensuing seasons. It was probably as much down to two big ankle injuries that he suffered as it was to the unimaginative crash-ball style of the Sharks, where he was paired in the midfield with Trevor Halstead.

When weighing up the Boks' achievements on their end-of-season tour in 1997, Rossouw believes that perspective should be kept because of the gulf in quality that existed between the hemispheres at the time.

"The introduction of the Super 12 in 1996 resulted in a big improvement in rugby in the Southern Hemisphere. As a result, we were far ahead of the Northern Hemisphere," he says.

Even so, the rout of France in Paris was a remarkable performance, which was crowned by Rossouw's individual feat.

"I don't really think about that anymore. In fact, this interview is the first time it has been raised in depth. Perhaps the fact that I was fairly new in the team at the time resulted in it not being particularly imprinted in my memory," he says.

"You don't realise on the day what a privilege it is to be there. There are a lot of things that need to go your way during the game for you to be able to score four tries.

"I felt there were other matches in which I played just as well, if not better, but didn't score as many tries. However, people tend to use tries as a measure of performance."

Much like Joel Stransky with his famous drop goal in the 1995 World Cup final, the four tries is not something that Rossouw dines out on.

"It's a distant memory now . . . one for the scrap book," he says.

It's certainly a scrap book that will make for enjoyable reading when he opens it for his children and grandchildren one day.

Beating the All Blacks

"Today's the day that we've got to decide whether we want to be world champions or not."
- NICK MALLETT

To think a retirement village now stands at the scene where Pieter Rossouw glided through the All Blacks' defence to land the killer blow in South Africa's memorable 13-3 victory at Athletic Park on 25 July 1998.

Pope John Paul II once dropped in for a visit, while pop star David Bowie and rock group Dire Straits performed there in the 1980s.

It is fitting company for Rossouw when one recalls the stunned silence that descended on the scene as the Springbok wing planted the ball under the posts after a dummy conjured up between himself, flyhalf Henry Honiball and scrumhalf Joost van der Westhuizen.

With Rossouw's try – converted by fullback Percy Montgomery – South Africa landed the decisive blow in an epic arm wrestle.

The Springboks had been 3-0 up at half-time and coach Nick Mallett made a dramatic plea:

"Today's the day what we've got to decide whether we want to be world champions or not."

Of course, they were officially world champions thanks to the World Cup triumph in 1995, but it was clear from their matches against the All Blacks in 1996 and 1997 that South Africa wasn't the strongest team in the world.

Mallett's team heeded the plea.

Rossouw's was the decisive moment in a test that up to that point could have swung either way as South Africa had a slender 6-3 lead.

The All Blacks now found themselves 10 points down with just 10 minutes left. There was still enough time, but by then the Kiwis had arrived at the conclusion that there was no way through and were a dispirited bunch. Ed Morrison's final whistle put them out of their misery.

It is a victory that will resonate as among the Springboks' most famous, not least because it was the first time since South Africa's return from sporting isolation that they were able to beat the All Blacks in New Zealand.

The previous Springbok victory in New Zealand had been in 1981 – also at Athletic Park – with a team captained by Wynand Claassen prevailing 24-12.

By contrast, the 1998 match was played in the context of political legitimacy. The Springboks were the most welcome of tourists and were attracting media attention for all the right reasons.

Furthermore, the victory was achieved less than a year after the Boks had been slaughtered 55-35 by the All Blacks at Eden Park in Auckland. It highlighted the dramatic turnaround that had been brought about through the astute guidance of coach Nick Mallett and a fine management team, which included the likes of Alan Solomons (assistant coach), Jake White (technical advisor) and Rob van der Valk (commercial manager).

But it also highlighted just how foolish it can be to enter a test of such magnitude without a reliable goalkicker. All Black coach John Hart had made a huge selection blunder by picking Carlos Spencer at flyhalf ahead of Andrew Mehrtens.

Spencer was a gifted playmaker but his inclusion always came packaged with an element of risk.

Mehrtens was the man for a tight test. He had the ability to dictate the course of a match and a boot that marked him as one of the game's finest goalkickers.

To illustrate the point, Spencer had fluffed five penalties by the time he was replaced with Mehrtens – to a loud cheer – in the 48th minute.

While Hart played his part in crafting his own doom primarily through picking Spencer, he also had the difficult task of reshaping the All Blacks after iconic figures Sean Fitzpatrick, at hooker, and No 8 Zinzan Brooke, had called time on their test careers.

Loose forward Taine Randell was Fitzpatrick's successor as captain and history will attest to the fact that it was a difficult period for the Kiwis.

The tension at All Black training sessions in the build-up to the test against the Boks had been tangible in the wake of a defeat to the Wallabies.

With their team consistently returning a win ratio in excess of 80%, New Zealanders are understandably not schooled in the art of tolerating defeat.

But a combination of their coach's poor selection combined with the genius of Rossouw and Honiball, and stoic Springbok defence, brought them down in Wellington.

The move for Rossouw's try had been crafted by Honiball on the flight to New Zealand from Sydney. He had been challenged by Mallett to think of something and came up with a move that the Auckland Blues once did that confused him.

In the words of Rossouw: "I stood at the back of the scrum. The ball went from Joost to Henry, who took it flat. I then received the ball from Henry and ran through the space that opened up between them to score under the posts. I remember how the stadium went dead quiet.

"When I called the move, Percy didn't actually know what to do. He had forgotten it! I just told him to go to the blind side and it actually helped because it created uncertainty among the All Blacks.

"It was one of the most satisfying tries I scored in my career. I always got a bigger kick out of making tries than scoring them, but that one left me with an unbelievable feeling."

The Boks had first practised the move on the Wednesday before the game and repeated it later. Of course, execution in match conditions is another matter, but between Van der Westhuizen, Honiball and Rossouw the Springboks were in safe hands.

"Pieter's timing is an example of how he could hit the line at just the right time and place. Henry attacked Josh Kronfeld and Joost drew Mehrtens, which allowed Pieter to just cut through like a knife through butter," Mallett recalls.

"The silence in the stadium as he scored was incredible. It was almost as if everyone had held their breath. I heard the referee's whistle as clear as if he had blown it on the Rondebosch Common.

"The only thing I heard from the crowd was a New Zealander next to me saying 'oh shit'!

"It helped us that Carlos Spencer missed a few kicks, but we finished well. We could actually have beaten them by more. There was a break through the middle and it was only nervousness that prevented us from finishing it off."

Rossouw believes the selection of Spencer over Mehrtens was a determining factor.

"We played into the wind in the first half and Spencer missed those penalties. If Mehrtens had been in the starting line-up, we probably would have lost," he says.

"We had to defend a lot, but it worked. As the match progressed, the All Blacks did not want to attack the 10/12 channel with Henry and Pieter Müller there anymore."

The Boks had lady luck smiling on them throughout the course of their Tri-Nations tour. They had beaten Australia 14-13 in Perth before travelling to New Zealand and it was in no small part thanks to Wallaby fullback Matt Burke missing four out of five kicks at goal.

"It was a good Australian team, with the core of the side that won the

World Cup a year later. They had good players and coaches," Rossouw says.

"Burke missed from in front of the posts on our 22-metre line. The reality of rugby is such that everyone would have spoken about how wonderful their performance had been if he succeeded with the kick."

Mallett was uneasy about the quality of the Boks' performance in Perth and made no bones about it as he addressed the media in Wellington in the build-up to the match against the All Blacks.

"The more I watch the video, the worse it looks. It was our second poorest performance that year. I thought that the one against Ireland (the Springboks had struggled to a 37-13 win over a sub-standard Irish team in their first test of the year) was our worst.

"Both ourselves and the Wallabies would have lost by 20 points against the All Blacks with the way we played on Saturday."

The Boks had a slight disruption on the eve of the match in Wellington when flank Rassie Erasmus had to withdraw from the starting line-up due to an abscess on his shin. He was replaced by Andrew Aitken, who played exceptionally well in a team that heeded their coach's call for a dramatically improved performance.

"I remember afterwards that Henry Honiball was walking around the showers in the change room, so I asked, 'What are you doing?' He just said, 'They can't take this away from me, they can't take this away'. I said, 'What are you talking about?' and he said, 'I'll go to my death bed knowing that we had earned this," Mallett recalls.

A testimony to the Boks' defensive effort is that they had lost the match in every facet barring the scoreboard.

Statistics were published in a New Zealand daily newspaper that showed the All Blacks had the ball for eight minutes more than the Boks.

The Kiwis also dominated territory and were thwarted in spite of having nine scrums in South Africa's half and big guns such as Walter Little (centre), Christian Cullen (fullback), Jonah Lomu and Jeff Wilson (both wings) to break them down.

Müller's 20 tackles were the most in the game, while Aitken (13), lock Mark Andrews, No 8 Gary Teichmann and Honiball (all 10) also worked hard on defence.

Outside centre André Snyman and Van der Westhuizen were South Africa's most prolific ball-carriers, making 45 and 43 metres respectively.

But the All Blacks also dominated that area, with Little (75 metres), Randell (58 metres), Lomu (57 metres) and Mehrtens (40 metres) all making good yardage.

But somehow the Boks kept them out.

"Geesh they tackled . . . Hell we played well," Mallett marvels years after the event.

"Andrew Aitken made an important tackle on Christian Cullen in the last few minutes. Cullen had stepped off his left foot and it was something we had spoken about before the game.

"Cullen didn't step off his right foot much. He's very quick and was racing down the touch line. Aitken was there and he smashed Cullen as he stepped inside."

That piece of calculated defence said it all.

With their mission in the Antipodes having been accomplished, the Boks travelled back to South Africa with a swagger. The most difficult part of the campaign was over and they had set themselves up for Tri-Nations glory by bagging eight log points overseas.

However, the Tri-Nations would be a fight to the finish and not dependent on the Boks' next match against the All Blacks in Durban. Australia had beaten New Zealand 27-23 in Christchurch the week after South Africa's triumph in Wellington.

The Aussies scored four tries in the process and were two log points ahead of the Springboks before the South African leg of the tournament.

But the Boks were still in pole position. If they beat the Kiwis in Durban, they would enter the final weekend either two or three points ahead at the top of the table.

South Africa's victory at Kings Park on 15 August 1998 is one that will always be spoken of for the Boks' remarkable fight back in the final 12 minutes, in which Van der Westhuizen, replacement loose forward Bob Skinstad and hooker James Dalton all scored tries to clinch the game 24-23.

It was a Lazarus-like stunt after they had been down 23-5.

While South Africans were understandably euphoric afterwards, and the team's reputation grew, Mallett had a different perspective at the time.

"What was a pity about that is that we had played so well away from home. Perhaps we didn't play that well in Perth, but we won a close game 14-13 and it was a key moment in the development of our team as we had beaten a decent Australian side away from home," he says.

"With the All Blacks having lost to Australia, we knew the final would be at Ellis Park (against the Wallabies a week after the match against New Zealand in Durban). So it wasn't a case of us beating New Zealand and then being champions.

"It was the only time I saw our team a little tentative. The players went on in that first half thinking that they don't want to miss the final with an injury instead of putting their hearts and souls into the game."

The Boks' ears were ringing after Mallett's half-time talk – they turned at 5-17 down – but there wasn't any immediate effect as Mehrtens added two more penalties on top of scrumhalf Justin Marshall and Randell's first-half tries.

"I remember climbing in and having a full go at half-time, but that wasn't what changed the course of the game. What changed it was the impact players we sent on and the message to Gary Teichmann: 'Don't even kick for touch. Just play.'"

The term "impact players" was coined by Mallett, who saw his substitutes bench as a critical element and used it to particularly good effect. His ace was the wonderfully gifted loose forward Bob Skinstad, whose ability to conjure up something special was unrivalled in world rugby at the time.

Then there was loosehead prop Ollie le Roux, whose giant frame belied his pace.

"Ollie would play so well for the 30 minutes he got that there would be pressure for him to start. But he would make the same amount of tackles in those 30 minutes that he would over 80 minutes in a provincial game," says Mallett.

"He would carry the ball for us and smash people. I was getting a fantastic game out of him, as I was from Robbie Kempson or Os du Randt when they started before him.

"When I put Bob on, I would move André Venter to lock. That gave us huge attacking ability because Venter would never stop running and before the switch I had gotten 50 minutes out of Andrews.

"Andrews got cross because he didn't want to go off, while Venter didn't want to move to lock. But Venter would make as many tackles at lock as he did at flank.

"Franco Smith could also go on and he was perhaps more of a passing centre than Müller, while Aitken was a creative player.

"If you were down, those guys could really make a difference if they were sent on."

With their half-time deficit of 5-17 having grown to 5-23, Mallett rang the changes during the second half of the Durban encounter.

Skinstad replaced lock Krynauw Otto as early as the 40th minute, Le Roux went on for Adrian Garvey in the 52nd, and Aitken and Smith replaced Rassie Erasmus and Snyman, respectively, in the 64th.

With Le Roux on in place of Garvey, the versatile Kempson could simply move over to tighthead prop.

"The guys just upped the tempo in those last 20 minutes. The other teams weren't making similar use of their bench, so it was a big advantage to us. I just chucked the guys on and said that we should attack at every opportunity and play quick tap penalties.

"We scored three tries in that period and that was fantastic, but New Zealand had also become conservative. They thought that they couldn't lose from the position they were in. Instead of sustaining their attacks and holding onto the ball, they kicked it to us. We had possession for those last 15 minutes and New Zealand just imploded."

South Africa's first try in their fightback started with an attack by Honiball down the blind side. He was brought down, but the All Blacks were penalised for off-side on their 10-metre line.

Montgomery kicked for touch to set up a lineout about 15 metres from the All Blacks' try-line. Dalton found Teichmann at the back of the lineout and the Boks mauled it up.

As the ball came out at the back from Dalton to Van der Westhuizen, the scrumhalf glanced to his left as if readying himself to feed his backline. It was enough to divert the All Blacks' attention and, with their focus on his outside, the scrumhalf cut through the first line of defence and beat a despairing tackle to score under the posts in the 68th minute.

The conversion was over, but the Boks were still very much fighting an uphill battle at 12-23 down.

It didn't take them long to score their next try. The All Blacks knocked the ball on after chasing their kick-off and, from the resultant scrum, Honiball broke and ran through to the visitors' 22-metre area but the ball was lost forward.

Marshall cleared well from the base, but the resultant lineout was the perfect attacking platform for the Boks. Honiball attacked the line with Skinstad then taking on the defence before popping the ball back to Smith.

Aitken was next to scoop up the ball after it had been planted by Smith and the Boks drove relentlessly through the middle.

The ball was recycled at the back of the ruck and spread to Stefan Terblanche on the outside. It came back inside to Teichmann, who was brought down a metre short. It then travelled via Van der Westhuizen and Honiball to Skinstad, who finally scored the try.

With the two points added, the Boks were in with a sniff at 19-23.

But South Africa nearly committed suicide shortly thereafter when Montgomery made a mess of fielding a kick just metres from his goalline. He recovered, but passed to Rossouw under pressure. The lanky wing was himself caught and could do nothing else than concede a 5-metre scrum.

New Zealand attacked from the base, but the ball was turned over with some courageous defence. South Africa then defied every rule in the text book when they attacked from the scrum on their 22-metre line. The Kiwis were penalised at the ensuing ruck and then marched back for another 10 metres.

Müller then charged forward, but his pass went forward off a team-mate's legs. Cullen then launched the ball into the Boks' 22-metre area. Rossouw tapped after calling the mark and countered his way through some heavy traffic before off-loading in contact to Müller. The centre found himself in the clear, but was brought down by Cullen.

But the scrum was awarded to the Springboks and the ball was spread wide to Terblanche, who tried to kick it down the touchline. The ball went directly out, but Lomu was late with a tackle on the Bok wing.

The penalty on the All Blacks' 22-metre line set up the perfect attacking opportunity for South Africa. They set up a lineout about five metres from the All Blacks' try-line and drove over for Dalton's try.

There was still time for another kick-off and play, but the Boks shut the All Blacks out with aggressive defence. As the final whistle went, the Kiwis were in dire straits on their try-line.

It was a fightback that would go down as one of the greatest between tier-one countries in the history of the game.

Whether Dalton really "scored" that last try has been a talking point ever since. Mallett smiles when he recalls the episode.

"He tried to rip the ball out of Aitken's hands because he wanted to score himself. Had he just pushed Aitken over, the try would have been scored. I have a sneaking suspicion Dalton may just have lost control as he went over," says the coach.

"Dalton was a very competitive guy. He didn't lose too many games for the Springboks. He was hard and nuggety. I kept him disciplined by saying that I would take him off if he conceded too many penalties."

According to Rossouw, the belief that had been fostered among the group came through strongly in the 24-23 victory.

"We were probably not in the right mental space for the game, but the experience was there to pull it off even if things didn't go our way," he says.

"It was a special test. There was a momentum shift, with us starting to get breaks and half breaks. The substitutes did well for us. As a team, we had the confidence to kick for touch from penalties. You back yourself when you are on a roll."

Did he think the match was beyond the Boks' grasp at 23-5 down?

"I always believe there is a chance. I knew the clock was winding down, but that there would be a chance if we could score a quick try."

Mallett does not believe the tremendous fightback was necessarily the result of the team's great character.

"I think the players realised how lucky we had been. I said to them afterwards in the dressing room that it wasn't just a case of us playing well. It had also been them playing badly," he says.

"New Zealand had been on the cusp of a win, but didn't know how to win the game and tried to play out the time by kicking the ball away.

That amounted to giving us possession. We then played really well because they were so nervous that they didn't want to lose the game."

Mallett then issued this warning to his players ahead of the next weekend's finale at Ellis Park: "If we play like that, we will lose to Australia."

The players didn't let him down, with a superb try by Skinstad in which everyone through to the great Wallaby centre Tim Horan bought the dummy, crowning the victory.

"The wake-up call against New Zealand was very good for us. We really cleaned up Australia (by 29-15). There was never any doubt about who was going to win."

South Africans probably considered the victories over the All Blacks as more significant than winning the Tri-Nations itself.

Luck had played its part, but the Boks had again established themselves as international rugby's premier side. In doing so they also gave the country the emotional lift that comes with beating their fiercest foes.

South Africa now had more to show than just a World Cup trophy which they had captured and would hold until 1999. They were unofficial world champions as well, which meant the worthiness of their official title was no longer beyond doubt.

CHAPTER 7

A Memorable Post Script

"You are never going to change Jannie . . . But I tell you he can do
things that Henry Honiball can't. He is a fantastic kicker of drop goals".
– BRENDAN VENTER TO NICK MALLETT

The year 1999 will go down as a bit of an *annus horribilis* in the history of
South African rugby, but it was lit up briefly in spectacular fashion by the
unlikeliest of heroes: Jannie de Beer.

He was the kind of flyhalf Springbok coach Nick Mallett didn't want at
the time. The coach had been spoilt with Henry Honiball in 1997 and 1998
and could build an impressive attacking game off the flat-lying flyhalf.

De Beer took the ball a little deeper, which stifled the Boks' ability to
score tries. But on 24 October 1999 De Beer gave his riposte: five drop goals
in a memorable World Cup quarter-final at the Stade de France that gave
South Africa a sensational 44-21 victory over England.

England had been the favourites and were expected to de-throne the
world champion Springboks. But there was a strong resolve in the Springbok camp and they had hatched a master plan that De Beer could execute with precision.

The moment was all the more special given all the drama that had
preceded it in 1999 – a poisonous cocktail of bad selections, political
interference, injuries and the sacking of Gary Teichmann as Springbok
captain.

Perhaps the single biggest moment that destroyed team spirit was
Mallett's decision to axe Teichmann ahead of the home leg of the Tri-

Nations. The hangover of the shock decision was still carried into the World Cup.

Mallett's plan was for Bob Skinstad to play No 8 in South Africa's defence of their crown, but the incredible thing was that he was still injured when the call was made on Teichmann.

To his credit, Mallett would later admit that he had acted in haste and it's unfortunate given his impressive legacy that he has been forced into that admission so often.

The disturbance that Skinstad's presence had brought to the side since 1998 was also more a result of the special talent he had been blessed with rather than due to anything Mallett did.

Skinstad had a strong personality and his boyish good looks sparked what would later become known as "Bobby-mania", in particular among female admirers. His ability to attract headlines more than any other player would irritate team-mates. It is a fact that South African rugby players respect bleeding for the cause considerably more than they do a sleight of hand.

But he was a trump card that worked a charm off the Springboks' substitutes bench until Mallett finally made the fateful decision that he should be elevated to the starting line-up at the expense of iron man André Venter for their test against Scotland at Murrayfield on 21 November 1998.

The Springboks won 35-10 and equalled the world record of 17 consecutive test victories at the time with a 27-13 win over Ireland at Lansdowne Road the following weekend. However, they went down 7-13 to England at Twickenham on the final game of their tour.

With that, Mallett's Springboks of 1997 and 1998 had to be content with sharing the record of 17 consecutive test wins with the All Blacks, whose sequence started in 1965 and ended in 1969.

More significant, however, was the fact that the Springboks' team dynamic had been disturbed.

Mallett was spared some difficult calls in the early stages of the 1999 season as Skinstad had sustained his knee injury in a road accident during a Super Rugby tournament in which he had been in exceptional form.

But another challenge emerged for the coach as pressure to transform his lily-white team began to encroach.

After a build-up featuring high political drama, the last all-white Springbok starting line-up played in the 19-29 defeat to Wales on 26 June 1999 at the opening of the Millennium Stadium in Cardiff.

Thereafter Mallett succumbed to the pressure to find a way to accommodate either Breyton Paulse or Deon Kayser in the starting line-up at the expense of one of his preferred wings, Stefan Terblanche and Pieter Rossouw. Terblanche ended up being sacrificed.

Injuries were also increasingly taking their toll. Mallett was without his first-choice halfback pairing of Joost van der Westhuizen and Honiball as the Tri-Nations kicked off for them with matches against the All Blacks in Dunedin and the Wallabies in Brisbane.

Teichmann captained the Boks in their first Tri-Nations match of 1999 – a record 0-28 defeat against the All Blacks at Carisbrook – and wouldn't play for his country again after that.

Rassie Erasmus briefly took over the captaincy for the following week's record defeat of 6-32 to Australia in Brisbane.

An increasingly under-fire and jittery Mallett had by now decided to hitch his wagon to Skinstad as his No 8 for the World Cup, even though the player had not yet made a recovery from his knee injury.

The axe fell on Teichmann and Van der Westhuizen was installed as captain for the home leg of the Tri-Nations. The scrumhalf himself was only just returning from a major injury.

But there still wasn't a sign of the man Mallett said was the first one he penned onto his team-sheet: Honiball.

In his absence, Mallett juggled Gaffie du Toit and Braam van Straaten as flyhalves before De Beer became available and played in the 10-9 victory over Australia at Newlands. The narrow victory mercifully closed the book on a horrible Tri-Nations campaign.

And so South Africa limped off to the World Cup. There was little hope of Honiball being fit for their opening group match against Scotland. Skinstad was still nursing his injured knee, consistency of selection had dissipated, confidence was low and team spirit was in tatters. It seemed like a recipe for an early exit.

Mallett had no other choice than to retain De Beer in his starting line-up for the opening game, which ended up being an impressive enough 46-29 win over Scotland. Some of the gloss was taken off that triumph by unimpressive victories over minnows Spain (47-3) and Uruguay (39-3). When the calculation was made, England were the favourites for the quarter-final in Paris.

Mallett was a worried man. He would not have Honiball fit, while inside centre Brendan Venter had been red-carded against Uruguay.

Venter was no more than a little reckless in his rucking, but he was suspended for the match against England and Pieter Müller would have to wear the No 12 jersey.

Venter nevertheless still had a big role in crafting South Africa's victory.

The drop goals were his idea, while Müller also ended up being an important player in executing the plan. "I must give credit to the players. It was Brendan Venter who came to me," Mallett recalls.

"We were playing golf on our off day and I was in the same four-ball as Brendan.

"I said to the guys in my caddy cart that I was concerned that we weren't going to score tries. Jannie plays it so deep and we're not getting the ball on the advantage line like we did with Henry. Our backs aren't getting across the advantage line, which isn't allowing our forwards to get into play.

"Brendan said 'You are never going to change Jannie. You can't make him play like that, but I tell you he can do things that Henry can't. He is a fantastic kicker of drop goals'. He hasn't kicked a drop goal in this World Cup because he thinks it's not our game plan'."

Mallett was open to the idea and was encouraged by Venter to speak to De Beer.

"I went to Jannie and remember asking him where he liked kicking drop goals from on the field. Some guys, for example, like it on the left-hand side of the field. They take the pass there and then look up. Naas Botha used to kick a lot of his drops off lineouts from the left-hand side.

"Jannie liked to take it straight back in the centre of the field from a scrum. So we worked out moves to take the ball up through the middle. It didn't matter if we didn't get much go forward. It just had to come straight back."

If the Boks needed affirmation that it would be the right tactic, De Beer provided it in training with 10 successful drop kicks from as many attempts.

"I couldn't believe it. We came off that field and I said to him, 'Listen, if we get into any good position, don't worry about tries, have a crack'."

The Springboks didn't have it all their own way in the quarter-final against England. They were harshly dealt with by Scottish referee Jim Fleming in the first half and couldn't get into the right field positions to execute the plan.

Nevertheless, the Boks took a 16-12 lead into half-time following a try in the left-hand corner by Van der Westhuizen. Fleming awarded it on the advice of the touch judge.

Flyhalf Paul Grayson drew England within one point shortly after the restart, but the Boks started exerting some physical dominance and could increasingly rely on set-piece ball in the English half.

De Beer would soon dampen any enthusiasm generated by Grayson's penalty as the Springboks increased their advantage on the back of England's mistakes and set the stage for De Beer's drop goal show from the 43rd through to the 74th minute.

The first came after England fullback Matt Perry's decision-making had let him down when he ran a kick by fullback Percy Montgomery up from his 22-metre area.

England lost possession after Perry was tackled by Montgomery and André Venter took the ball up on the left-hand side of the field. It came out to Van der Westhuizen and he passed it back sharply to De Beer in the pocket.

The drop kick went over without De Beer being under significant pressure and the tactic had clearly caught England by surprise.

De Beer's second – two minutes later – was once again punishment for poor decision-making by England that led to them conceding turnover possession. South Africa had been penalised for infringing after England launched a lineout drive. There was no need for anything rash, but rather than do the logical thing by setting up good field position with a kick to touch, England took a tap.

Possession was lost and Springbok outside centre Robbie Fleck countered up field. The ball was recycled and then went out to the left, with flank Rassie Erasmus taking it up. Os du Randt found himself in the unfamiliar role of scrumhalf off that phase and flung the ball out to his left before it came back inside to De Beer – right in the middle of the field where he had told Mallett he wanted it. He made no mistake.

De Beer's third was set up by the simplest of moves. Müller simply took the ball up from a solid scrum in the middle of the field and it came back to De Beer from Van der Westhuizen.

It was pretty much the same recipe for the fourth – a scrum on the right-hand side of the field, Müller taking it up and Van der Westhuizen passing back to De Beer.

The fifth was the most impressive of the lot considering the distance – it was kicked from between the halfway and 10-metre line, slightly to the right of the field. This time a lineout was the platform, with the ball coming back to De Beer after it had been taken up.

De Beer then added two penalties before launching a high cross-kick which bounced awkwardly and was snatched by Rossouw for a try that would be the final insult.

De Beer's conversion was his 12th successful contribution with the boot and brought the score up to 44-21. His contribution was a remarkable 34 points through five drop goals, five penalties and two conversions.

The devout Christian thanked his Creator afterwards with a famous line quoted in the *South African Rugby Annual* of 2000: "The Lord gave me the talent and the forwards gave me the ball."

His quote spawned the memorable "The Boot of God" headline in the *Express*.

De Beer mentioned in an interview with the *Cape Times* years later that they hadn't expected the drop goals to play such an overwhelming part in the victory.

"The first two were from turnovers and not actually planned. After that the guys started calling and planning it. Everything just happened for me on the day," he said.

"I was a bit shocked. You walk off and are on cloud nine for a few days. It wasn't like I felt I was the main man. It worked in one game, but it was not to say it would work in the next.

"I had attempted a lot of drop goals in my life and wasn't convinced they would go over. It just happened.

"Afterwards I said I just want to honour God for giving me the talent and there were lots of stories in the newspapers."

Asked whether he prayed to win, De Beer answered in the negative.

"No. I said we had managed to beat England and I want to thank God for the ability and talent. If you lose and you have given everything, that is fine. Then it's not a case of God not being on your side anymore. Christianity is for everyone, not just for South Africans."

Significantly, the Springboks had also just about managed to get over the Teichmann issue. There was a good bonding session over a few beers between the players after the struggle against Uruguay and they were out to make the most of the opportunity that presented itself.

"It was a really tough year, but we all go through those," Mallett reflects.

"What really turned it for me was the win against England. We had played well against Scotland, but didn't smash Spain and Uruguay as we should have. But we really played well against an England side that was convinced they would beat us. It had a lot to do with the tactics we had taken into the game, combined with the motivation of the team.

"There was a good feeling in the side because our preparation for the World Cup had been good.

"When I saw Jannie kick those drop goals in training, I knew he would be influential. I knew the English defence was well-organised and they were a metre back from the last man's feet. They were careful not to concede penalties and were very disciplined in defence.

"I just felt that our ability to score tries would depend on them making mistakes because our backline wasn't firing with Jannie at flyhalf. Once we started kicking those drop goals, they were forced to start playing with the ball more and made mistakes.

"Our preparation for that game had been outstanding. We knew exactly how England would play. Lawrence Dallaglio (No 8) had a key role as ball player, and they would kick the ball miles down field after setting up in the middle."

De Beer, of course, would not have been able to achieve his feat without a strong showing by the Springbok forwards. They were magnificent on the day.

South Africa's first phases were solid, while the ball came out as cleanly as Van der Westhuizen could have hoped for at the back of the oven. Naturally the quality of the possession was a great help to De Beer.

"Our forwards were always dominating, but we weren't going to score tries because our backline wasn't exerting enough pressure with the ball in hand. But Jannie was knocking them over and England realised they were not going to win by sitting back and defending. They had to play and our defence was very good at the World Cup," says Mallett.

Brendan Venter's intervention and Mallett's willingness to listen to that kind of input highlighted one of the team's biggest strengths. Notwithstanding the whole Teichmann drama and the injury to Honiball, Mallett could still rely on a number of intellectuals in his squad. His management style also meant that the players were sufficiently empowered to offer their input.

"I believe I always had a good relationship with the players in the sense that I took a lot of pleasure from drawing information from them in terms of moves or defensive patterns," says Mallett.

"Brendan even at that stage was very astute and Rassie was way ahead in terms of interpretation and analysis. Henry could come up with moves that teams would struggle to defend.

"It's absolutely crucial to your people-management that you allow players to come up with ideas and then try to incorporate it if it can work.

"As soon as a player comes up with something and you incorporate it, he also feels obliged to get it right because it was his idea."

Perhaps Mallett had missed Honiball so much that he was a little harsh in his original assessment of De Beer prior to that incredible game in Paris.

The flyhalf's record – at Free State and ever since he made his test debut in the third test against the British and Irish Lions in 1997 – suggested he had all-round qualities as a flyhalf.

But it's his boot for which De Beer will be remembered, in particular on that remarkable day at the Stade de France.

Mallett was not sold on the same tactics doing the trick against Australia in the semi-final, but a fit Honiball felt it would be wrong for him to start the match.

"Henry said that I couldn't change the team and that I should keep Jannie for the semi-final," Mallett recalls.

"I knew that I may need a more defensive player in the team. There was no comparison between the two defensively. But Henry said it would be wrong to change."

De Beer was again South Africa's most important player against the Wallabies. He kept his head to slot a penalty that forced the game into extra time, where the Springboks were ironically sucker-punched by Stephen Larkham's famous drop goal. South Africa lost 21-27.

Having scored all of South Africa's points in the semi-final, there would again be no justification to drop De Beer for the play-off for third place against New Zealand. But De Beer effectively axed himself to ensure that Honiball could play one last game for South Africa.

"Jannie came to me straight after we had lost and said 'I think Henry should be able to bow out by playing in the last game, so please don't pick me'," Mallett recalls.

"It just shows what fantastic people we had playing for South Africa. The two of them were absolutely gentlemen. They are wonderful people and we can be incredibly proud of them.

"I can't think of any other team sport where a guy will give up his place for another member of the squad. Just think of the unselfishness.

"Henry had never played a World Cup game. He was injured before the first one and he was basically knocked out of the semi-final by Jannie's performance.

"He could have gone through his career never having played a World

Cup game. But from a team point of view it was his belief that Jannie should continue. And then Jannie, to his great credit, realised that the team needed something to pick itself up.

"They were so depressed about losing that semi-final and Jannie felt the only way we could do it was to make it a dedication in which no-one would let Henry down. And no-one did. They played absolutely brilliantly in beating the All Blacks 22-18."

And so a rollercoaster World Cup campaign – and season – ended on a poignant note as De Beer and Honiball both bowed out in a manner befitting their ability and personalities.

There was to be no South African fairytale as in 1995, but certainly a memorable post-script to a turbulent season.

The Robbie Fleck Show

*"I just think the players at the time weren't capable of playing
the style he wanted. We were pretty set in our ways. It ultimately led
to Nick's demise and unfortunately so."*
— ROBBIE FLECK

It would be a triumph in anyone's language to beat the mighty All
Blacks 46-40, but the writing was already on the wall for Nick Mallett's
Springbok coaching career by the time the home leg of the 2000 Tri-
Nations came about.

South Africa had done pretty well with a third-placed finish at the
World Cup in 1999, but Mallett felt that the Springboks' playing style
would have to be adapted to ensure they stayed in touch with the
modern game.

Going down that route has always been a dangerous game for Springbok coaches. Carel du Plessis did it before Mallett and Harry Viljoen after
him. It ended in tears on each occasion.

Mallett also had the problem that he would be forced to make important personnel changes after the World Cup.

Henry Honiball, who was the key man in Mallett's back line during the
glory days of his tenure in 1997 and 1998, called time on test rugby after
the play-off for third place at the World Cup.

He left a void that was only periodically filled with conviction in the
ensuing decade.

Braam van Straaten was the flyhalf in all but one of the eight tests under Mallett in his final year. He had done well over two seasons for the

Stormers in the Super12, but was a metronomic goalkicker rather than someone who could spark the attack.

Goalkicking, of course, is an essential skill, but Mallett's best games were built around Honiball, who took the ball flat and orchestrated the Springbok attack.

Mallet's other option in 2000 was Louis Koen, who also wasn't his coach's cup of tea and was regarded as a potential weak link on defence.

The coach had had to cut his suit according to his cloth at the previous year's World Cup while Honiball was recovering from injury.

He had known that Jannie de Beer didn't offer him the flat-lying threat of Honiball, but with the help of Brendan Venter he arrived at a game plan in which the Springboks would sink England with drop goals in their quarter-final.

But that party trick was a one-off and a home series against a tough England side loomed large.

"We scored a lot of tries when I started coaching the Springboks in 1997, but weren't significantly better than our opposition in 1999 and couldn't replicate that. Sometimes we got a little too conservative," says Mallett.

"When 2000 came, I just decided that we were going to give ourselves the opportunity of scoring more tries and I was going to pick players capable of doing that."

The negativity of 1999 was now something of the past and the opportunity was there to start from scratch.

Mallett kicked off the year with a training camp in Plettenberg Bay where he could test some of his new ideas in practice sessions.

The Super12 earlier that year was a major influence. Until their defeat to the Crusaders in the final, the Brumbies had set the pace with their dynamic play with the ball in hand.

It was based on building continuity through passes and dummy runners that were often used to beat defences.

Mallett was eager to incorporate the new attacking trends into Springbok rugby.

South Africa beat Canada easily enough by 51-18 in their first test of the year, but the path ahead would be a difficult one. There were seven consecutive matches against top opponents in England, Australia and New Zealand ahead.

It was a programme that would leave any coach with sleepless nights and certainly not the kind of opponents against whom you want to test a new playing style.

While South Africa won their first test against England at Loftus 18-13 – ironically thanks to six penalty goals after all the fuss over a more attacking style of play – the wheels came off afterwards.

The games in which Mallett's plans took a big knock were the second test against England in Bloemfontein and, straight after that, the inaugural battle in the Nelson Mandela Challenge Plate against Australia in Melbourne.

South Africa initally competed well in both, but the concern about both defeats – 22-27 to England and 23-44 to the Wallabies – was the extent to which they were second best.

Against Australia, the Springboks were up 23-20 before conceding four tries from the 67th minute onwards. Their forwards had also been dominated by the English and it was a controversial try by Joost van der Westhuizen seven minutes from full-time that brought respectability to the scoreboard.

That was enough to get the publics' backs up and, when the Springboks lost 12-25 to the All Blacks in Christchurch and 6-26 to the Wallabies in Sydney, the knives were out.

Predictably, New Zealand were considered the overwhelming favourites for South Africa's first home game in the Tri-Nations at Ellis Park on 19 August 2000.

But a twist of fate in the build-up strengthened the Boks' hands dramatically, though they wouldn't know it until game day.

De Wet Barry, who had been pencilled in to play inside centre, was ruled out with a hamstring injury. Robbie Fleck was then recalled after the axe had fallen on him in the wake of the disastrous tour Down Under and he was asked to play out of position at inside centre. Grant Esterhuizen would be the man on his outside in what seemed a bizarre make-up for a midfield.

"I had seen Fleck play for the University of Cape Town and Western Province. I always thought he was a better outside centre with a creative player on his inside. But South Africa didn't have that many creative ones at the time," says Mallett.

"Fleckie was very different to a crash-ball player. He beat people with his feet. But we got the ball to him earlier. If you put him at inside centre, he could beat people for dead. I watched him play touch rugby and he was a little like Breyton Paulse. They could beat people without being touched."

As it turned out, Fleck produced one of the most impressive individual performances against the All Blacks in the post-isolation era. The fact that he played out of position ended up being a blessing.

South Africa produced a relentless attacking performance and it was right wing Chester Williams who was first on the scoreboard after the ball was floated to him inside New Zealand's 22-metre area. The World Cup hero cut inside to beat the last defender before grounding the ball.

Then came the Fleck show.

The Springboks made another foray deep into All Black territory before striking. The ball came out from a ruck on the left side of the field and after receiving it from flank Rassie Erasmus after play moved to the right, Fleck broke the line superbly to score the try.

"I got an early ball and spotted Andrew Mehrtens and Pita Alatini (the All Black flyhalf and inside centre respectively) close together. Alatini was drifting off and I just stepped and went between them and scored," Fleck recalls.

"As an inside centre you want the ball early so that you are able to attack the advantage line. There was no way I was going to pass that ball. It was a situation where I was going to have a full crack."

South Africa then conceded a turnover try to All Black right wing Tana Umaga before Fleck pounced again. This time the ball was turned over at a ruck and Fleck broke inside to notch his brace.

"I remember Taine Randell and Ron Cribb (flank and No 8 respectively) drifting too far. I cut inside them and then went outside again before I had a free run to the try-line," says Fleck.

"For me the first try was the special one because it was a new experience playing inside centre and I was in the perfect position to score."

Fleck was also involved with incisive runs in the build-up to both scrum-half Werner Swanepoel and fullback Thinus Delport's tries that gave the Boks a commanding 33-13 lead.

"I recall doing that quite a few times in that game," says Fleck.

"It's probably not normal for an inside centre to look for an outside gap. They are usually required to straighten and pass. I just got a lot of space and it worked out nicely."

But Fleck's heroics almost proved to be in vain as the All Blacks hit back with tries by fullback Christian Cullen and Umaga. By half-time they were very much in it at 27-33 down.

Flyhalf Braam van Straaten increased the Boks' lead to 36-27 after the restart, but after a converted try by Cullen and a penalty by Mehrtens the visitors suddenly led 37-36. They had scored 24 points against three and had the bit between their teeth.

It evolved into a see-saw game, with Van Straaten regaining the lead for the Boks with a penalty before Mehrtens edged the All Blacks ahead again with a drop goal.

However, Swanepoel had the final say and, after the Boks had launched a foray deep into the All Blacks' 22m-area, the scrumhalf squeezed through a visibly tired Kiwi defence to strike the knockout blow.

According to Fleck, the Springboks hadn't specifically planned their attack around him.

"Obviously I was ecstatic about my call-up. Nick said to me that I was going to have a crack at playing inside centre. My response was that I hadn't played there since my school days and obviously it was going to be very different at test level," he says.

"It was a great opportunity for me. It allowed me to get my hands on the ball earlier. I could already feel the enjoyment in training. I was going to bring something different to the table to what the team was used to.

"I knew that Mehrtens and Alatini weren't great defenders, but there wasn't a specific plan to have a go at them.

"Nick said that we had to go out there and express ourselves. I just played what I saw in front of me and fortunately they were pretty weak in that area."

Fleck had distinguished himself as a fine outside centre earlier in his career, but was so good in the No 12 jersey against the All Blacks that it seemed as if he had missed his vocation.

"I would have loved to play inside centre more often," he admits.

"You must have a special skills set to play inside centre. The modern day No 12 needs to be able to kick and pass like a flyhalf. He must be able to dominate the collision like a loose forward, make his tackles and get stuck in at the breakdown.

"I wasn't the most physical guy and didn't have a great pass, but one thing I could do was create space for others. I played two more games for South Africa at inside centre after that, but would have loved it to have been a lot more.

"Tim Horan (the great former Wallaby No 12) always said that he felt

I was an inside and not an outside centre. That was a compliment, but it was probably too little and too late. I should have started playing there earlier on in my career."

Does Fleck on reflection consider the win over the All Blacks as the greatest game of his career?

"There were many I enjoyed for various reasons, but I loved that game for the enjoyment factor – the amount of space I had and my impact on the game," he says.

"Perhaps the main reason I remember it so fondly is that just prior to that I was pretty much out of the Bok set-up. I had been dropped and thought that was it for my Springbok career. That game was almost like a fightback to get back to the top. It just showed a bit of character."

Mallett reckons the 46-40 victory was born out of his team finding its feet in executing his vision.

"New Zealand had a fantastic team, with Umaga, Cullen, Jonah Lomu, Justin Marshall and Mehrtens all playing. We played really well," he says.

"It was certainly a game where I felt we were approaching a well-balanced style of play. We were as attack-minded as we were defence-minded.

"We also played really well in my last game against Australia. But for a poor decision by the referee penalising Corné Krige when he should have nailed Joe Roff, and an absolutely fabulous kick by Stirling Mortlock, we would have won."

But the Boks lost 18-19 to the Wallabies in Durban to make it three defeats out of four Tri-Nations games. With the defeat to Australia for the Nelson Mandela Challenge Plate and the shared series against England factored into the equation, it amounted to just two wins in seven games.

Did Mallett perhaps take the Boks too far out of their comfort zone by attempting to change the way they played?

"No, I knew it was the way to go," he says.

"I also knew we didn't have as strong a side as in 1997. I was picking players who weren't as skilful. Braam van Straaten, bless him, wasn't as skilful as Honiball. And Werner Swanepoel wasn't a Joost van der Westhuizen.

"Joost was a world class player, but picked up a bad injury. Henry Honiball was hard to replace at flyhalf. We had guys like Gaffie du Toit and Braam van Straaten. They had different qualities. I think Braam showed the ability to handle pressure better than Gaffie in test matches, certainly defensively.

"It was working though and I was finding a new team. It was interesting that when the team was taken over by Harry Viljoen and Rudolf Straeuli, the results were very poor.

"It wasn't a great era of South African rugby from 2000 onwards. Sometimes you are blessed with the era you get. Jake White inherited a very good group of under-21 players and he had the skill to mould them into a very good team. That side was then inherited by Peter de Villiers.

"The proudest thing I could say is that no-one had scored 46 points against the All Blacks. And no side had scored six tries in a match against them. We did it with a backline of Werner Swanepoel, Braam van Straaten, Robbie Fleck, Grant Esterhuizen, Chester Williams, Breyton Paulse and Thinus Delport."

Notwithstanding Mallett's claims of having turned things around, the Springboks' performance should be seen in perspective. South Africa are known to produce backs-to-the-wall jobs in pressure tests at home.

The fact of the matter is that South Africa failed to score a single try in four of the eights tests they played under Mallett in 2000.

André Vos had been appointed to succeed Van der Westhuizen as captain, with the latter having done a stand-in job after Teichmann was sacked.

Was Vos an inspirational leader? Harry Viljoen certainly had his doubts after succeeding Mallett and axed Vos to appoint Bob Skinstad as his skipper.

Nevertheless, a lot of South African rugby's problems on the field from 1999 through to 2003 often stemmed from the lack of a flyhalf with x-factor.

Interestingly, Jaco van der Westhuyzen made his test debut deep into the Boks' win over the All Blacks. He would later be given ample opportunity by Jake White to establish himself in the No 10 jersey, but didn't pass the test.

Casting the debate of Mallett's game plan aside, he definitely didn't deserve the sack considering what he had achieved earlier in his tenure as Springbok coach.

But by then he had fallen foul of rugby officialdom and, in truth, not even a victory over the Wallabies after the one over the All Blacks would have rescued him.

The wheels were set in motion to work him out of the system, even though his players were quite clear that he should stay and wrote a letter to Sarfu to that effect.

It was to no avail and published remarks by Mallett over his views that ticket prices were too expensive were seized upon by Sarfu to call him to a hearing for a violation of the governing body's code of conduct.

It turned into a media circus and the whole affair culminated in Mallett and Sarfu parting ways.

"Quite frankly, I had been taking flack since the beginning of 1999. The win over New Zealand was a nice way to end and it was a great pity that we lost to Australia," says Mallett.

"I was pleased to be able to walk away on the back of a really good performance. And it wasn't an unhappy team. I think 20 of the players wrote to Sarfu after the test against Australia saying they would like me to continue as coach.

"But it wasn't going to work out. There were all sorts of other things that happened at the time. The comments I had inadvertantly made to a journalist gave Sarfu the opportunity to act against me."

Fleck says the team felt the pressure on the coaching staff at the time, especially as rugby officialdom was not united behind Mallett.

"The selectors and coaches were almost bargaining who they could have in the side. It was getting to a situation where the pressure was really on Nick and his coaching staff, as well as on the team. And unnecessarily so," he says.

Does he think Mallett was perhaps taking the Boks down the wrong path?

"Nick had to make some changes to keep us in step with the modern game. Maybe he tried to change things too rapidly. One thing I can say is that Nick is one of the best coaches I ever had and he wouldn't have done it for any other reason than to improve Springbok rugby.

"I just think the players at the time weren't capable of playing the style he wanted. We were pretty set in our ways. It ultimately led to Nick's demise and unfortunately so."

South Africans would only realise in the ensuing three years that it was a big mistake to get rid of a Springbok coach with a winning record in excess of 70%.

Neither Viljoen nor Straeuli after him could get to grips with the job.

Mallett probably did get it wrong in 2000, but would have had the savvy to turn the ship around.

Nevertheless, a coach is ultimately only as good as his players and one inspired performance belied the fact that he just didn't have a good enough team.

CHAPTER 9

Selection Shenanigans

*"I wanted to play Fourie, but they wanted to make sure there were
enough players of colour in the team. At that point my selection had to
go via the team manager and the Saru president. The message back
was that they wouldn't accept it."*

— JAKE WHITE

Sometimes the extraordinary is achieved under extraordinary circumstances and South Africa's 40-26 victory over New Zealand on 14 August
2004 was a prime example.

This was the first year of Jake White's Springbok coaching tenure, having succeeded Rudolf Straeuli in the wake of the disastrous 2003 World
Cup campaign.

And it wasn't even so much about South Africa crashing out at the
quarter-final stage as it was about the drama that had preceded the tournament. The headlines were dominated by an ugly racial incident in
which bearded Blue Bulls lock Geo Cronjé had allegedly refused to share
a room with coloured Western Province second-rower Quinton Davids.

And, of course, who will ever forget Kamp Staaldraad, where leopard-
crawling in the nude was among the Springboks' team-building activities!
Funny as that sounds now, it wasn't back then, considering everything
that had gone before, during and after.

White was given the difficult task of rebuilding Springbok rugby and
expectations were so low that Ireland were favoured to win the first test
of his tenure in Bloemfontein.

Of course, such pessimism was never warranted. The Boks won the
series 2-0 with victories of 31-17 in Bloemfontein and 26-17 in Cape Town.

After that they beat Wales 53-18 in Pretoria before heading Down Under for what would always be the real test.

A comfortable 38-24 victory over a combined Pacific Islands team followed in Gosford (76 kilometres north of Sydney) before the Springboks headed over to Christchurch for their test against New Zealand.

And controversy struck in both weeks.

First of all there was a little drama in Gosford, where White sent home Victor Matfield after a diagnosis of a knee injury. There were strong rumours at the time of a personality clash between them. Gerrie Britz was then picked as No 5 lock in Matfield's place.

Then, as if to prove a point about his fitness, Matfield ran out in a Currie Cup match for the Blue Bulls against the Lions the following weekend. It was the same day on which the Springboks played the All Blacks in Christchurch and Albert van den Berg had in the meantime been called up after Britz sustained an injury against the Islanders.

Van den Berg's call-up, in itself, was a controversial one as he was promoted over the head of Davids into the Springboks' starting line-up for the test against the All Blacks.

White's explanation was a simple one: Davids was a lock in exactly the same mould as No 4 Bakkies Botha. He needed an athletic No 5 lock to complement his bruiser. It was a solid rugby argument and may have sufficed had there not been a racial dynamic and, of all people, Davids being the victim.

The coach won the battle, but would later lose a similar one before picking his team for the Ellis Park clash against the All Blacks.

While the Springboks lost 21-23 to the All Blacks in Christchurch, it probably represented a significant turning point in South African rugby and indeed the immediate rivalry between the two rugby giants.

The match was a thriller, with the Boks succumbing to a late try by All Black right wing Doug Howlett. South Africa had posted all their points in a first half in which left wing Jean de Villiers scored a try just 23 seconds into the game.

The Boks followed that up with another heart-stopping loss against the Wallabies in Perth the following week. It was another right wing – former South Africa under-21 international Clyde Rathbone – whose late try condemned the Boks to a 26-30 defeat this time.

But on both occasions there was honour in defeat and a statement had been made. White's Boks had proved they could mix it with the big boys and in the process bagged two crucial bonus points.

It was akin to a draw and there were home matches against New Zealand and Australia on the horizon.

South Africa's chances of winning the Tri-Nations were then strengthened when the Wallabies beat the All Blacks 23-18 in Sydney. The Springboks now had to do their bit by winning both of their remaining games.

Significantly, South Africa's lineouts had been a shambles in Perth after a fit-again Britz was recalled in place of Van den Berg. White therefore had little choice but to call up Matfield for the Ellis Park showdown with the All Blacks. It would be cutting off his nose to spite his face if he didn't.

But that little sideshow was the least of his problems. By now the new coach's honeymoon was over and the net of racial politics was increasingly encroaching. This time White did not win the round as he did in Christchurch.

White relented after getting the message from the South African Rugby Union (Saru) that there weren't enough players of colour in the team he wanted to pick for the Ellis Park match.

The coach had to make a sacrifice and it was scrumhalf Fourie du Preez who had to make way for Bolla Conradie.

"I wanted to play Fourie, but they wanted to make sure there were enough players of colour in the team," White recalls.

"At that point my selection had to go via the team manager (Arthob

Petersen) and the Saru president (Brian van Rooyen). The message back was that they wouldn't accept it. I'm not sure who exactly decided that."

While such uniquely South African situations always have an unpleasant and unfair feel about them, it wasn't a train-smash for the coach.

White decided to get his "numbers" right with a change at scrumhalf, as Conradie was a quality player in any event. But it nevertheless sent the wrong message as Du Preez had trained as the starting scrumhalf for the entire week.

Had it not been for that change, tighthead prop Eddie Andrews and right wing Breyton Paulse would have been the only players of colour in the starting line-up.

The three in the starting line-up satisfied the rugby bosses, while there was a fourth player of colour on the bench in hooker Hanyani Shimange.

"Not picking Bolla to begin with wasn't as a result of me thinking he wasn't good enough. I wanted to pick Fourie because I thought he was better," says White.

"I thought that the one area I could change that didn't seem that significant at the time was scrumhalf. Remember that Fourie was a youngster at the time and not yet the player he would become by 2007.

"So from a coaching point of view it was easier to shuffle the scrumhalves and use Fourie as a substitute than to make a significant change at prop, among the loose forwards or on the wing.

"Bolla was playing well enough and I wasn't too uncomfortable about picking him. Looking back now, it put a bit of pressure on me in the long run. Fourie always felt that I hadn't treated him well there.

"I just didn't feel it was the right thing to tell him at the time. I don't think it would have been fair on either Bolla or Fourie. It would also have been unfair on the selection process as people would then have questioned every decision I made on the basis of whether it was forced or based on gut feel."

And so the Springboks ran onto the field with a side that satisfied the politicians and still had White believing they could win.

There was a little bit of panic though as things threatened to go pear-shaped early in the game. The Springboks were down 10-0 after just 10 minutes following a penalty by All Black flyhalf Andrew Mehrtens and fullback Mils Muliaina's converted try.

But what followed was a special bit of South African rugby history as centre Marius Joubert became only the second Springbok of all time to record a hat-trick of tries against the All Blacks. Winger Ray Mordt was the first at Eden Park in Auckland on the controversial tour of 1981, though South Africa lost that test 22-25 in spite of his heroics.

The first got the Boks back into the game. Eighthman Joe van Niekerk picked the ball up at the base after a powerful scrum close to the All Blacks' goal line and attacked on the blind side, where he found Joubert. The explosive Bok centre then slipped All Black captain Tana Umaga's tackle, scored and triumphantly threw the ball into the ground. Right wing Breyton Paulse was the first to arrive to hug the man who scored the try that crucially reduced the deficit to three points.

Joubert's second try started with a similar build-up – a scrum followed by a Van Niekerk pick-up and an attack down the blind side. He slipped Mehrtens' tackle and the Boks drove through the middle before recycling and moving the ball down the line.

Joubert's centre partner, De Wet Barry, was the creator this time. He spotted his opposite number, Sam Tuitupou, checking Joubert's run and attacked the space on the All Black midfielder's inside. Barry had also beaten a despairing dive by openside flank Marty Holah and, after being caught by Muliaina, off-loaded to Joubert. Montgomery converted and with 31 minutes played the Boks were suddenly leading 19-13.

Joubert's third try clinched the game. The Boks were leading 33-26 with less than five minutes left. Once again a scrum deep in All Black territory was the platform from where the Boks attacked. This time it was Jacques Cronjé, who had replaced Van Niekerk at No 8, that attacked off the base.

He tied up Mehrtens and Umaga before flipping the ball to Joubert on his inside. The last All Black in Joubert's path had been wrong-footed and the explosive centre touched down under the posts with All Black lock Simon Maling managing no more than getting his fingertips on the try-scorer. Joubert was swamped by team-mates offering their congratulations and the lasting scene was that of him and wing Jean de Villiers counting to three on their fingers and embracing.

"That was just something that happened on the spur of the moment and certainly wasn't aimed at rubbing New Zealand's faces in it," recalls Joubert.

"Jean just came over to me and we counted spontaneously. I will always remember that. The youngsters at the Sharks, who were in their teens at the time, would come over to me and count on their hands for a bit of fun." At the time of this interview, Joubert was in the twighlight of his career at the Sharks.

For Joubert the day would be memorable in more ways than one. Nelson Mandela had greeted the players prior to the game and did more than shake the centre's hand. The great man also noticed a battle scar.

"I had a big cut on my nose from the previous game and he said, 'You got a big knock on the nose'. It was just nice that he took the time to say that."

For Joubert the try where he beat Umaga was the highlight of his performance.

"Tana was the All Black captain and a player of immense stature. The fact that I scored after shaking him off was incredible for me," he says.

But Joubert's reflection on the game is a humble one. He points out that his achievement would not in any way have been possible if team-mates had not created opportunities for him.

"Joe van Niekerk was a big threat from the base of the scrum and gained good yardage. De Wet Barry and I had also come a long way. I knew that he was a hard and direct runner, and that I should run on his shoulder. I had a feel for what he would do and he also knew how to find me.

"The pleasing thing that day is that my all-round game was good. I had a big hand in creating a try for Jean as well."

Joubert is also full of praise for White's coaching role.

"The two bonus points we managed to get on tour gave us a chance. Jake motivated us with a very positive speech. He maintained from the outset that we could beat New Zealand. His point of reference was that some of our players had done it at under-21 level," Joubert recalls.

"He would also recall the history of the flour bomb test on the Springbok tour of 1981, tell us how tough it would be and that we would have to be on our game."

Mental toughness hadn't been a problem over the course of those incredible 80 minutes.

"We absorbed the pressure for the first 15 or so minutes and ultimately could probably have scored another three tries. We could have given the All Blacks 50," says Joubert.

White admits that he was deeply concerned when his side had conceded 10 points so early.

"When we were down 10-0 I thought, 'Here we go again'. I thought they were on a roll and could demolish us," he says.

"But I had seen some of the All Black players out the night before, walking around Sandton Square (Nelson Mandela Square). They looked a really confident bunch. It wasn't late, but I thought it a bit odd that they were out and about on the Friday night.

"All of our guys were in the hotel. I'd actually gone with the staff to get something to eat and saw the All Blacks sitting in the square there."

White made sure that there was sparkling wine in the team room once the Boks were back at the hotel. He then asked the players who had not previously beaten the All Blacks to stand up while the bubbly was being uncorked.

It was almost the entire bunch.

The significance of that cannot be overstated. Prior to this victory, South Africa had lost eight consecutive tests to the All Blacks. It was a slide that had to be arrested and this was a big turning point in the modern history of matches between these two rugby giants.

"It made the team realise that they are capable of beating the All Blacks," says White.

"We had been pumped by them for years. There was a stage in our history where we were ahead of them in terms of victories between the teams. Once they caught up they opened up a lead and it started getting a little one-sided (from 1999).

"The mere fact that players were toasting each other about the first time they had beaten the All Blacks was magnificent."

This victory came five days shy of four years since the Boks had last beaten their fiercest foes. That was the 46-40 victory at the same venue when Nick Mallett was still the coach.

White, in fact, was the third coach since Mallett walked the plank, with Harry Viljoen's and Straeuli's teams unable to take any All Black side far outside of its comfort zone.

There were eight players – Percy Montgomery (fullback), Schalk Burger (flank), Matfield, Botha, John Smit (hooker and captain), Os du Randt, CJ van der Linde (both props) and Du Preez – in the match-day squad of 22 who would eventually be in the starting line-up of the team that beat England in the World Cup final of 2007.

The question is why Joubert didn't see the journey through. His performance at Ellis Park in 2004 had been a testimony to his immense talent and he was among the nominees for the award of the International Rugby Board's player of the year in 2004.

"I think it was more of a mental thing than skill-related," says White.

"I would always challenge Marius and ask him at what point he was going to become a senior player and a go-to man.

"I thought at the time that the hat-trick would make Marius realise just how important he was to the team. But it wasn't to be. He just never ended up becoming the player that everyone thought he would. Marius had all the skills, but couldn't lift himself up that one level.

"No All Black had ever scored three tries against South Africa, so that puts into perspective what a massive achievement it was."

Joubert has a different perspective, pointing to being picked out of position in a struggling Stormers side in 2006 as one of the reasons for his and Barry's eventual departure from the Springbok side.

"Of course I'm disappointed that De Wet and I didn't push through. The problems had their origin at the Stormers, where I started getting picked on the wing and De Wet at outside centre. Jean got to play in his preferred position at inside centre," says Joubert.

"Consequently I couldn't sustain my form. You really only play well in the position you are familiar with.

"Jean and Jaque Fourie ended up playing very good rugby in the Springbok midfield and deserved to stay there."

Joubert, at least, was left with a lifetime's memories and a painting of him and Mordt adorns a wall in his home.

The significance of the game went beyond the victory and breaking of a mental barrier. White was re-shaping the Springbok team and had embarked on a process that he firmly believed would culminate in a final victory at the 2007 World Cup in France.

And he was staying true to South African strengths in the process.

The fact that Joubert's tries had their origin from the base of a powerful scrum was no coincidence. Du Randt was on skipper John Smit's left in the front row and would continue as first-choice loosehead prop through to the World Cup final.

South Africa's turnaround had been incredible. Just over a year previously they had lost 16-52 to the All Blacks at Loftus. Furthermore, there was a happy ending to the political side of things.

Mandela and the Finance Minister at the time, Trevor Manuel, had both been in attendance.

They related to Springbok rugby in different ways. Mandela was its biggest friend and gave unconditional support, while Manuel had been on record as saying that he was an All Black supporter.

The latter was in line with the resistance of many black rugby enthusiasts prior to the fall of Apartheid.

But Manuel shared the Springboks' joy, and on the evening of 14 August 2004 switched his allegiance.

Asked by the author of this book – writing for the *Cape Times* at the time – whether he was now a Springbok supporter, he was emphatic in his reply: "Yes."

Considering everything that happened the previous year and in the build-up to this test, it was a remarkable turnaround for the week to end on a note of political harmony.

But that's the South African melting-pot for you.

CHAPTER 10

The Magnificent Matfield

"Thankfully Victor was such a special player that it was abundantly clear to Jake that he was the best No 5."
– JOHN SMIT

Jake White was one of a number of dads watching their sons playing rugby at the Diocesan College (Bishops) in Rondebosch when the text messages started flooding in. Australia had kept alive South Africa's Tri-Nations dream by beating New Zealand 23-18 in Sydney.

The Springboks trailed both the All Blacks and the Wallabies by seven points on the log (two against nine) after the match, but if they won their two home matches handsomely enough they would be crowned champions.

Of the text messages it's the one from his captain, John Smit, that he can recall vividly. He said: "You won't believe it. Australia have won. That means we will win the Tri-Nations."

Had New Zealand won that match, the Tri-Nations would effectively have been over as they already had eight log points before kick-off – three ahead of Australia and six ahead of South Africa.

The prospect of winning the tournament with two matches left was all the incentive a hungry young side needed to restore the image of the battered Springbok brand in the wake of all the controversies of 2003.

White's side had set about their task purposefully by achieving one of the great historical victories over the All Blacks down the years, but the Wallabies would pose a unique challenge in the Tri-Nations finale.

The Wallabies were a more physical side than they would be in the ensuing years and could still bank on the direction provided by the formidable halfback pairing of George Gregan and Stephen Larkham.

"Australia were tougher competition than New Zealand for us that year. They were a harder team to play and, of course, still had Gregan and Co. They still had unbelievably experienced players," recalls Smit.

"Gregan was almost a team on his own with his intelligence, playing style and ability to gather people around him. They were also a smarter team than the All Blacks. They played us better, so we would have to think on our feet for that test."

White's recall of lock Victor Matfield for the home leg of the Tri-Nations would end up being of particular significance as South Africa probably would not have won the tournament otherwise.

Matfield delivered a man-of-the-match performance in the decisive 23-19 victory over the Wallabies on 21 August 2004. He dominated the line-outs and scored the try that swung the match early in the second half.

This was after White's medical staff sent him home during their tour for an examination of an "injured" knee. Matfield played for the Blue Bulls on the same weekend that South Africa squared up to the All Blacks in Christchurch, suggesting there were differing views on whether he was indeed injured.

In his absence, both Albert van den Berg and Gerrie Britz were tested – and found wanting – in the No 5 jersey.

With regard to the much-publicised personality clash between White and Matfield, the coach said his decision to call up Van den Berg was partly a bit of people-management.

"It's significant that Victor was the man of the match in both the World Cup final of 2007 and the match that clinched the Tri-Nations in 2004. It shows how good he was, but also that he had to be managed," says White.

"Victor was one of those players who liked to do things his way and didn't really like it when a coach pulled in the reins. At that time he was also injured and I wasn't going to take a risk.

"He was told by the medical staff that he wasn't going to play (against a combined Pacific Islands team in Gosford). He played for the Blue Bulls and was poor. I then brought him back because I realised I needed him.

"If he was fit enough, he could play. I was never going to drop him on performance. He was only going to get dropped if he was injured. But I think he also realised then that he had to start playing well."

White was also keen to create competition for the No 5 jumper. He had a number of candidates for the No 4 jersey, but beyond Matfield not much in the way of potential lock partners for the likes of Bakkies Botha and Quinton Davids.

"I brought in Albert to create pressure in the position. I didn't want a situation where Victor thought he had an easy road to selection.

"My point is that Victor probably didn't take kindly to that because he felt like he had an open-ended ticket into the team. The pressure I created was something that he had to control and work with.

"I wasn't trying to be a smart-ass. I needed to create pressure for that No 5 jersey. We didn't have competition for the position of the tall, athletic, jumping lock. I had plenty of the bashing, direct, ball-carrying locks that could jump at the front of the lineouts."

Smit has a different perspective on the issue and described White and Matfield's relationship as a "work in progress" all the way through to 2007. He also believes that White was concerned that Matfield had designs on his position as captain.

The coach was always unshakeable in his belief that Smit was the right leader for the side and had gone as far as making the captaincy appointment even before the international season had kicked off.

It was a move for which White copped a lot of criticism because it rendered the performance of all of South Africa's other hookers in the 2004

Super Rugby tournament irrelevant regarding potentially making the starting line-up. They could not make the side as long as Smit stayed fit.

But White was a coach with a plan and he would always stick to it.

Smit believes that Matfield would have been quite capable in the role of Springbok captain – as the great lock would later prove himself to be – but at the same time he never felt threatened. In fact, he believed that Matfield's exceptional talent would be an important element in the side and fought for his selection.

Smit describes White as an "old school" coach, who was also irritated with the lock in his mind for being something of a fancy dan.

"I think he sometimes misunderstood Victor. Victor was a natural born leader in his own right and could easily have done the job of Springbok captain. But it was either his hair, the colour of his boots or something else that irritated Jake.

"I literally had to fight for his selection on a weekly basis. Thankfully Victor was such a special player that it was abundantly clear to Jake that he was the best No 5.

"The first two years were definitely the hardest because Jake felt Victor spelled trouble. I wanted Victor in the team.

"Jake is so old school. It was how he created his career as a coach. He wanted to make a statement and teach Victor a lesson.

"So Gosford I doubt was about a knee injury. It was probably about setting the tone and showing who is boss. At the back of Jake's mind it was probably a situation of 'Victor will be my 5. Let me just show him . . .'."

Intriguing as the entire debate about the White-Matfield relationship is, it is with hindsight neither here nor there. Matfield delivered in a big way against the Wallabies and would never look back in his Springbok career.

While Matfield was often unfairly criticised for being too loose by old school critics, he was a formidable combination of an outstanding ball player and lineout genius.

Matfield maintained his remarkable presence up until his last test for the Springboks against the Wallabies in the World Cup quarter-final of 2011.

It would be churlish of even his harshest critic not to want to congratulate him for his performance against the Wallabies in 2004.

And, surprisingly – or perhaps not so much in the South African context where grinding players command disproportionate respect compared to the more skilful ones – there were many of those.

Such criticism is often based on the simplistic argument that a forward should not be in the backline.

But why should a forward not be allowed to make a contribution in broken play and why inhibit a gifted player from displaying his skills with the ball in hand?

As it turned out, Matfield picked up South Africa's Try-of-the-Year award for the touchdown that swung the match early in the second half.

He beat Gregan by feigning a pass to lock partner Bakkies Botha on his outside and then cut inside to score and give South Africa the lead. This was after right wing Breyton Paulse had won back his own high kick. Percy Montgomery converted and with the lead of 10-7 came a surge of confidence on the back of the terrific try.

Earlier, the Wallabies' South African recruit, Clyde Rathbone, had been instrumental in crafting a try that saw the Aussies go into the break with a 7-3 lead. His grubber kick was grabbed by fellow wing Lote Tuqiri, who cut inside and beat Paulse and flank Schalk Burger before scoring.

But the controversy of Rathbone crossing over to the Wallabies had not yet subsided and, in front of a crowd that he would have been able to call his own in Durban, he made a number of errors under pressure.

South Africa were down 3-7 at half-time, with fullback Percy Montgomery having struck a penalty after Tuqiri's converted try.

Matfield's try just five minutes into the second half gave the Springboks a grip on the match that they would not surrender.

He also played a role in No 8 Joe van Niekerk's try 10 minutes later, after Wallaby hooker Brendan Cannon had been penalised with a free kick for a delayed throw. The ball travelled to the right and then back to the left before Matfield found Van Niekerk with the final pass.

Montgomery then added two penalties for a commanding 23-7 lead with just 18 minutes left.

But the final quarter would end up being anything but a cruise.

Apart from the Wallabies' fighting spirit, there were yellow cards issued by referee Paddy O'Brien in the closing stages to Montgomery and Paulse.

Montgomery was first sin-binned for tackling Wallaby fullback Chris Latham in the air in the 69th minute and mercifully returned just as Paulse got his marching orders for a professional foul.

The clock would tick on for an anxious 11 minutes from the time of Montgomery's yellow card, which proved the catalyst for the Wallabies' fightback. The Aussies had it all their own way in that period.

Larkham crafted their first try by delaying his pass behind a dummy runner and then floated the ball to ouside centre Stirling Mortlock for a terrific touchdown.

The second try was scored by flank George Smith from a maul off a lineout.

Time had just about run out after Matt Burke – on for Mortlock – missed the conversion attempt, but there was to be one more kick-off and play. The score was 23-19 to South Africa and a try would clinch it for Australia.

"I still remember Gregan coming to his try-scorer and saying, 'Let's steal it from them'," recalls Smit.

"That is what Australia were about at that stage. They were a relentless and never-say-die team. There was a lot of intelligence in their game and they had vast experience.

"It was probably our toughest match in the Tri-Nations that year. On top of that, Durban is the easiest venue for test opponents against us. It's just a friendly place and the people are very friendly in the week leading up to games. The crowd is very relaxed.

"We did not have the benefit of altitude, so we had to beat them by being a better team."

On the balance of play South Africa could certainly claim that they were. The match ended with one final Australian surge in which Smith's grubber went over the touchline. With that Australia's hopes of winning the tournament dissipated.

"I remember George Smith whacking the ground in disgust after he had kicked the ball and it went into touch. He realised how close they had been to winning it," recalls White.

The significance of the victory was also put into perspective for White by then Wallaby coach Eddie Jones, who would end up being a technical consultant for the Springboks at the 2007 World Cup tournament.

"Eddie told me it was the hardest loss he had to live with because they really needed to win it as well. It was almost a defining moment in his tenure as coach because they had come so close on a number of occasions," says White.

"They had just lost out to England in the World Cup final of 2003 and he said this Tri-Nations was a trophy they had thought they could win. He reckons that, if they had won it, they probably would have taken another step as a team.

"That is how significant it was to them. As it was for us as we won the Tri-Nations."

For South Africa the victory represented a remarkable turnaround after the disasters and scandals of 2003. The Springboks had all of a sudden been transformed into a side capable of beating the All Blacks and Wallabies.

South Africa's Tri-Nations campaign also shaped a new generation of Springboks. The forward pack in the victory over Australia contained five members – Smit, loosehead prop Os du Randt, Matfield, Botha and flank Schalk Burger – of the team that would start the World Cup final in 2007.

Smit naturally grew as a leader on the back of the win over the Wallabies.

"John had won the Junior World Cup as a captain and now he added the Tri-Nations to that. He then went on to win the World Cup. He was always going to be the captain," says White.

"It was never a difficult decision for me to make because the players looked up to him. He was the guy that his team-mates wanted as captain, irrespective of what people may say."

Smit would always have to prove to South Africans – and, as far as many are concerned, he never did – that he was the best hooker in South Africa. There would at different stages be clamours for Gary Botha, Schalk Brits and Bismarck du Plessis to wear South Africa's No 2 jersey ahead of him.

Nevertheless, the winning of the Tri-Nations put his impressive captaincy into perspective. His handling of the Matfield situation also spoke of maturity when lesser people might have felt too insecure to allow for strong personalities in the team.

The campaign would also be marked by an outstanding contribution by flank Schalk Burger, who was named as the International Rugby Board's and South Africa's Player of the Year for 2004.

Burger's remarkable work rate, sheer physicality and nuisance factor at the breakdowns outweighed the performances of Smith and Richie McCaw for the Wallabies and All Blacks, respectively.

"He was by far the best player in the world," White says of Burger.

"I've said it many times: He was the difference between winning and losing in the time that I coached. His work rate and the effort he put in amounted to having an extra player on the field.

"Of all the players I coached, he was the best because of the fact that he could change the outcomes of games in a similar way Jonah Lomu did for the All Blacks. The way the laws were scripted and applied at the breakdown allowed Schalk to be a match-winner for us."

The feel-good factor also helped to cement a symbiotic relationship between White and Matfield.

"Matches like that helped," says Smit.

"It created a good couple of months where I did not have to fight for Victor's survival in the team. And then obviously the more he played the better he played. Jake then realised that he's a player with x-factor."

Matfield attended the post-match press-conference with White and Smit.

The coach then made a point of addressing Matfield personally.

"You made a lot of people proud today," White told him before addressing the room.

"Coaching is also how you get through to people. He was the right choice as Man of the Match. We also give our own award and he got that as well. He was good in the lineouts and made some great tackles."

Matfield himself said that it was an "incredible feeling" to score any try for the Springboks.

"I was worried. There were a lot of stories and I felt that I had to prove myself. The spirit in this team is the best of any I have ever played in.

"My job is to control the lineouts. John threw the ball in very well."

The same could not be said of Cannon, whose delays in taking his throws saw the Wallabies lose their lineout ball on three occasions. It was testimony to Matfield's sheer presence.

"They felt the pressure and that is why it took them so long with the throw-ins," said Matfield.

Jones also showered Matfield with praise and would continue to do so in seasons after that.

"He brought a lot more tactical awareness to their lineout. He's a very good technician and tactician. He deserves his Man-of-the-Match award."

Jones was equally full of praise for the transformation that White had engineered for Springbok rugby.

"The Springboks are playing smarter rugby. They are doing the basics well and it's difficult to get your hands on the ball with two centres [De Wet Barry and Marius Joubert] and a loose forward combination that contest so well at the breakdowns," he said.

"The better team won. It's as simple as that."

South Africa were now Tri-Nations champions and they had a superb base to build from. The best years were seemingly yet to come.

History shows that it was hardly plain sailing from there. The Springboks faltered on their end-of-season tour and would have a nightmare in 2006 before ultimately winning the World Cup.

Matfield certainly played a big role in ensuring that White's tenure would end successfully. The coach will acknowledge that, just as Matfield should credit White on an honest reflection of how his career developed over time.

The fact that there was no looking back for Matfield's Springbok career from there onwards was probably just about as significant as winning the Tri-Nations.

Triumph and Tragedy

"One of Solly's attributes was that he was a fighter.
The saddest thing of all was to see that the fighting spirit had left him."
— EUGENE MAQWELANA

It was a beautiful spring day in Cape Town on 16 September 2004 when Springbok coach Jake White made a shock revelation after a training session at the Diocesan College (Bishops): Solly Tyibilika will be Schalk Burger's understudy as his No 6 flank.

By then it was almost six weeks since Tyibilika had last been in action for the Sharks in the Currie Cup, with one-cap Springbok Warren Britz having settled in as their preferred openside flank.

Earlier that season, Tyibilika had featured in four Super Rugby games as a substitute, playing second fiddle to Luke Watson.

White was unperturbed, saying that he didn't pick the provincial sides and wished that he could. And, sure enough, Tyibilika was in his squad for the end-of-season tour in 2004.

Tyibilika had made his mark at the Sharks in the 2003 Currie Cup, scoring seven tries in 14 games. A balanced view of the try-scoring tally should nevertheless be taken as he often finished off rolling mauls.

Notwithstanding his apparent fall from grace in Durban in 2004, Tyibilika made an impressive try-scoring test debut in the Springboks' last match of a disappointing tour against Scotland at Murrayfield.

But come the Super Rugby campaign of 2005, Tyibilika again found himself on the fringes, and starting five of his nine matches from the bench.

White was again unperturbed as he picked him as his No 6 flank for the first test of the year against Uruguay in East London – a victory of 134-3. Granted, it was a soft test that South Africa could have won with 14 men, but the fact of the matter is that Tyibilika was in the selectors' thinking.

Next up for South Africa was a home series against France, where honours were even at 30-all in the first test in Durban.

The second test – a 27-13 victory in Port Elizabeth – would be one of South Africa's most impressive performances of the season.

Yet it was also a week in which the Tyibilika saga took another strange turn.

This time White was put under significant pressure – the message came via team manager Arthob Petersen – to pick Tyibilika. It was even suggested that he should drop Burger, who was the reigning International Rugby Board Player of the Year.

It was crazy stuff considering that the winner of the two-test series would be determined by this match.

The strength of the opposition was also put in perspective by the fact that the Springboks could have lost the first test had France's replacement scrumhalf, Dimitri Yachvilli, converted wing Julien Candelon's late try. There were anxious moments as the kick bounced back off the upright.

But South Africa is a unique rugby environment and, says White, the dynamic at play was the passing of non-racial sports icon Dan Qeqe on the Monday before the second test.

Qeqe was a revered former administrator, who had brushes with apartheid authorities for campaigning for change in South Africa's darkest days. He was also a prominent Christian.

But while the Springbok camp paid its respects, it didn't stretch as far as convincing White that he should change his plan to stick with Burger as his No 6 flank. He had already announced the team the Tuesday before the test.

Another dynamic was that Tyibilika had strong links to the Eastern Cape. He had been a member of the Spring Rose Rugby Football Club in his formative years in Port Elizabeth. It also happened to be Qeqe's rugby home decades previously.

The Eastern Cape, in particular, has always been a rugby hot potato in the political sense. Up until the establishment of the Southern Kings – and before that the Spears – rugby in Eastern Province had been in ruins for well over a decade.

In 1999 Nick Mallett had lost some sympathy on the basis that he did not pick hometown hero Deon Kayser for a test against Italy, which the Springboks ended up winning 74-3 and wouldn't have been in danger of losing even if they had picked specialist props on both wings. Mallett was consequently viewed as being unnecessarily stubborn.

Equally, Heyneke Meyer didn't escape whispers for the fact that he failed to fully appreciate the talent of loose forward Siya Kolisi – another product of the Eastern Cape – in his first season in charge.

A fine opportunity to hand Kolisi a debut in the third test against England in the Friendly City was missed after Willem Alberts had been injured. Instead, Jacques Potgieter was drafted in to make up a brawny but ineffective loose-trio with Marcell Coetzee and Pierre Spies.

Kolisi's form in the 2012 Super Rugby tournament had warranted inclusion, but he ended up being no more than one of the six young hangers-on that had been invited to train with the Springbok squad during the three weeks of the England series. It was stated with their inclusion that they would not be considered for selection.

The squad and team selections were probably rooted in the discipleship of size.

However, White's dilemma seven years previously was a different one altogether and there were more aggressive and complex political forces at work. He had shown himself to be committed to the transformation cause in his first year in charge, but the pressure now grew in his second season. The coach was also growing increasingly frustrated by the interference.

White boosted the transformation quotient that week by selecting Lawrence Sephaka ahead of Eddie Andrews at tighthead prop and preferring Ricky Januarie to Fourie du Preez at scrumhalf.

Andrews, of course, was a player of colour himself, but the inclusion of an ethnic black player in Sephaka was of particular significance.

Neither of those changes had been politically motivated.

Sephaka's role was also not going to be one where he could hide. He would have to square up to highly-rated French loosehead prop Sylvain Marconnet.

But Os du Randt's withdrawal on the eve of the PE-showdown meant that the versatile Sephaka would have to move to the loosehead side of the scrum. There he would have the equally tough task of scrumming against Pieter de Villiers.

White had a lot of faith in Sephaka, whose development he observed at Springs Tech while in the employ of the Golden Lions Rugby Union.

The same applied to Januarie, who shared the scrumhalf duties with Du Preez during the course of the International Rugby Board's under-21 World Cup in Oxfordshire, England, in 2003. White coached the team, with Burger as his captain.

Sephaka had also played loosehead prop for the under-21 side that had won the Junior World Championship in 1999, with White as assistant coach to Eric Sauls.

So White was comfortable with what these players offered him at the time, even though subsequently Sephaka never reached his potential and Januarie failed to make the most of his career in South Africa due to his poor conditioning.

"Ricky and Fourie had always been competing for the same jersey. I go back to what happened in 2004 [when political interference prompted White to pick Bolla Conradie ahead of Du Preez] and I think Fourie in many ways thought it was history repeating itself," says White.

"But Ricky was brilliant as a junior. He obviously picked up a bit of weight and let himself go physically a bit. But as a junior he was outstanding.

"And there were times that we needed Ricky. Something people don't realise is that our penalty count was significantly reduced when Ricky played because he cleaned the ball so quickly at the breakdowns, so referees couldn't penalise us that much.

"I picked him based on the fact that I thought we could play at a fast tempo."

But dropping the world's best player to accommodate Tyibilika was not something White was willing to entertain.

"I said, 'You have to be kidding. I can't drop a guy like Schalk Burger.' The response was they felt it is the right thing to do politically. And I said, 'Guys, I'm not doing the right thing. We are picking a rugby team to win a test match'," he recalls.

"What happened then is that I told them they can't keep interfering with selections. Now they weren't just talking about the number of black players. They were asking that I specifically pick Solly. I said [that] I'm not going to play Solly and then they said they are always fighing with me about selection. Then I said that I can't hang around here."

There was speculation in the press on the morning of the test that White had threatened to resign because of interference with selection.

"I didn't threaten as in 'I'm going to resign'. I just said that I can't carry on in the job if there is going to be continued interference in selection."

Given the press reports on the morning of the game, the victory ensured that White had the moral high ground.

"There was this whole thing about it being the end. I was going to be fired and it was supposedly going to be the end of my career. So in the greater scheme of things it was a massive test for us," he says.

Who knows what might have been had South Africa lost the test. It certainly would have provided ammunition for White's enemies.

But, as it turned out, the Boks made nonsense of fears that they might lack focus as a result of the controversy. They produced one of their finest performances under White and anyone wanting the coach out based on that would have had to have his head read.

"Schalk was fantastic, Jean de Villiers was brilliant on the wing, Bryan Habana scored twice . . . I thought in many ways that we played better in 2005 than we did in 2004," White recalls.

Among the highlights was the Boks' dominant scrumming performance, with Sephaka more than standing his ground against the world class De Villiers.

"That was one of the best tests that Lawrence played for us. People were worried about our scrumming and how strong the French scrum would be. We actually scrummed bloody well that day," says White.

The fact that all three of the Boks' tries were scored by their wings – two by Habana and the one by Jean de Villiers – speaks volumes about those players and the individual brilliance and predatory instincts they brought to the game.

But each of the Boks' three tries were rooted in turnover possession.

Habana's first came after the Boks had won possession at a ruck – it was probably no coincidence that Burger's blonde locks were sticking out on the French side – and the ball travelled swiftly through the hands to fullback Percy Montgomery after he had joined the line.

Montgomery cut the line and Habana drifted inside from his wing to collect the pass after the fullback had drawn the last defender. Habana finished by diving over unchallenged under the posts.

De Villiers scored his try by knocking the ball out of French fullback Nicholas Brusque's hands in the tackle and catching it before racing away to score again under the sticks.

South Africa carried a comfortable 20-6 lead into half-time and Habana's second touchdown in the 47th minute effectively put the match beyond France's reach. This time it was one of the great wing's trademark intercept tries.

White was delighted with the manner in which the players executed his plan in the victory of 27-13.

"The way we mauled – not just from lineouts but also from kicks-offs and broken play – was very good. Any person who has watched enough test rugby will know that the reason we won is simple: the forwards laid the platform," he said.

"We scored two of our tries through our defence. Many people say that you can only play with the ball, but we played very well without the ball. We basically closed France off out wide and in the middle. All credit to the defensive line.

"I've got to say that I enjoyed that win more than most. The reason is that French rugby was strong. I'm not taking anything away from our Tri-Nations win (in 2004). The thing I was most proud of was that we came back after taking a lot of criticism for the 30-all draw.

"It was what test rugby is all about: hard, physical and uncompromising. We took the right decisions and the right options."

White had also achieved a resounding victory over the rugby politicos.

He further got a ringing endorsement from captain John Smit, who stated shortly after the game that White was "the best coach I have ever had".

"He's an unbelievable man and one only has to look at how things have changed over the past 12 to 18 months since he has been involved. I stand with him through thick and thin and I believe most players will as well. You cannot measure my support for him in words," Smit was reported as saying by the *Cape Times*.

Selection convenor Peter Jooste also pleaded for an amicable resolution.

"One wouldn't like to see a change of coaches now. We're on a nice wave. There's nothing in life that can't be debated and negotiated around a table," Jooste said.

The tale of the players of colour in the game and events off the field spoke volumes about South African rugby's wrestling with the issue of transformation.

It could have been the breakthrough game for Sephaka's Springbok career, but he only played seven more tests.

White believes Sephaka could have achieved more had he worked harder.

"I think Lawrence will admit that he didn't work as hard as he could have all the time. He got some good breaks in the beginning. I don't think Lawrence appreciated what he had and realised how hard he had to work for it. It was often a combination of raw talent and taking shortcuts that got him in that position," White says.

Januarie made the World Cup squad in 2007 and the following year scored a magnificent match-winning try for the Springboks as they beat the All Blacks in Dunedin for the first time.

But his subsequent years in South Africa weren't good. Apart from being arrested for driving under the influence of alcohol, his conditioning deteriorated.

Habana is more a case study of what is possible when players are exposed to the right environment. He grew up in a wealthy family and was educated at the King Edward VII School (KES). The environment was always there for his natural talent to flourish and he ended up as Springbok rugby's record try-scorer.

Tyibilika's tale was particularly sad.

The highlight of his career was no doubt an inspired first half in the Nelson Mandela Challenge Plate match against the Wallabies at Ellis Park later in 2005. But Britz was again the preferred No 6 at the Sharks for their Currie Cup campaign.

Tyibilika was mostly consigned to Vodacom Cup duty in the early stages of 2006 and made no more than three Super Rugby appearances. It didn't prevent him from featuring in three Tri-Nations tests in Burger's injury-enforced absence.

That was pretty much that for Tyibilika's test career.

His frustration at lack of game time prompted him to sign a contract with the Lions, which ended up being career suicide. Tyibilika was snubbed for Super Rugby and did not even feature in the Vodacom Cup.

He later made three substitute appearances in the Currie Cup and would play as many times for the Emerging Springboks in the International Rugby Board's Nations Cup tournament in Romania.

It wasn't all his coaches' fault and Tyibilika contributed to his own demise through disciplinary problems.

But the old chicken and egg analogy probably applies here.

His fall was incredible – from test to club rugby within the space of a year.

To its immense credit, the South African Rugby Players' Association (Sarpa) made an attempt to rescue the situation.

But the final straw for Tyibilika's Lions career came when he went to play for Spring Rose in an Easter Tournament while still contracted at the union.

Not surprisingly, the Lions initiated procedures to relieve him of his contract.

Tyibilika then had three seasons with the Border Bulldogs from 2008 through to 2010 before his career – and life – ended in Cape Town.

He had been handed an opportunity to play for prominent club side Hamiltons, but kept the wrong company and was shot in a shebeen in Gugulethu on 13 November 2011. Less than a month previously he and two friends had been arrested for possession of an illegal firearm.

So what does all that have to do with South Africa beating France in Port Elizabeth on 25 June 2005?

Perhaps it offers us an opportunity to reflect on rugby's political sideshows and its long-term impact on careers. Notwithstanding some of the doors that were opened for him, the question should be whether Tyibilika was ever given a chance to succeed.

He played well at times but on occasions, such as the week of South Africa's fine triumph over France, he was a political pawn. Were those pushing for his selection sincere about what they were doing or was it simply a calculated effort in the name of transformation to get at White?

And should Tyibilika ever have been anointed as Burger's understudy? Any viewpoint would be a subjective one, but the answer is probably no. Should Britz have played ahead of him given the circumstances? Again, the answer should probably be no. Tyibilika was denied the opportunity to disprove the scepticism.

He ended up being spat out of the system and had fallen out of love with the game by the time he was murdered.

His friend Eugene Maqwelana – at the time of writing Sarpa's Manager of Player Affairs – captured Tyibilika's broken spirit with these words: "One of Solly's attributes was that he was a fighter. The saddest thing of all was to see that the fighting spirit had left him."

CHAPTER 12

More Madiba Magic

"I remember the Wallabies' eyes.
They looked at him and thought 'oh geesh, him again'."
— JAKE WHITE

If there had to be a sequel for *Invictus* – the film about Nelson Mandela's so-called grand plan to use Springbok rugby to unite the nation – the plot line could easily be found in the deciding match for the Nelson Mandela Challenge Plate on 23 July 2005.

While the moment was nowhere near big enough to be able to bring people together as in 1995, a team selection with a record number of players of colour in the starting line-up and squad of 22 may briefly have changed perceptions of Springbok rugby among the masses.

There were six in the starting line-up: loosehead prop Gurthrö Steenkamp, tighthead prop Eddie Andrews, flank Solly Tyibilika, scrumhalf Ricky Januarie, and wings Bryan Habana and Breyton Paulse.

Another three – hooker Hanyani Shimange, utility prop Lawrence Sephaka and centre Wayne Julies were on the substitutes bench.

There had only been four in the squad of 22 when the Springboks lost 12-30 to the Wallabies in Sydney two weeks previously. The numbers in the preceding series against France were four and five in the tests in Durban and Port Elizabeth respectively.

Of course, the demographics of the team was nowhere near being representative of the South African population, but at least created a greater impression of accessibility in Springbok rugby.

It should really be down to provincial and regional teams to create a bigger pool of talent so that transformation can become a natural process rather than being measured in numbers every week.

The fact that the national selection panel has to pick from teams that are overwhelmingly white, together with the political baggage that rugby carries, results in the Springbok coach unfortunately being at the mercy of the numbers game.

Jake White therefore caught the rugby public and media by surprise with his team selection for this match. What made it particularly relevant and newsworthy was that the match would be a celebration of Nelson Mandela's birthday. He had turned 87 earlier that week.

South Africa were the holders of the Plate, but after the defeat in Sydney they would have to win in Johannesburg to retain it.

However, many supporters were sceptical about the team White had picked and didn't hold out much hope.

Coach Jake White insists it was the team he wanted to pick and that it hadn't simply been loaded with black players for the sake of the event.

South Africa would play Australia four times that season, twice for the Mandela Plate and on another two occasions in the Tri-Nations.

Together with two tests against the All Blacks, it amounted to a sequence of six tests against top-quality opponents inside the space of eight weekends.

The schedule demanded that White rotate players and it provided him with an opportunity to sort the wheat from the chaff.

South Africa's defeat in Sydney also demanded changes, though supporters were astonished by the extent to which White shuffled his cards.

Paulse came in on the right wing for Jean de Villiers, with the latter moving to inside centre in place of De Wet Barry. Jaque Fourie was a straight swop for Marius Joubert at outside centre, while Jaco van der Westhuyzen made way for André Pretorius at flyhalf.

The entire loose forward combination was reshuffled. White opted for a loose-trio of Joe van Niekerk, Juan Smith and Tyibilika to replace Jacques Cronjé, Danie Rossouw and Schalk Burger.

Steenkamp and Andrews were drafted in as props, replacing Os du Randt and Sephaka at loosehead and tighthead, respectively.

"It was all part of a plan drawn up well in advance", White insists.

"I planned it so that everyone who was on the fringes would get game time in that test. It wasn't a case of picking more black players for Mandela. It just so happened that it was fantastic for South Africa's image. Mandela arrived and we had exceeded expectations in terms of transformation," he says.

If the media and the public were caught off-guard by the selection, the players certainly weren't.

"I told the guys that because of the long season they would play in certain games. All the guys who started were aware that they would play in that game," White says.

"Not only were they mentally prepared but, as a team, they had also run together quite a bit. We would spend additional time after training sessions in the run-up to games to practise with a team that would play further down the line. There was a bit of added work done."

The obvious significant advantage the Boks held was that the match would be played at Ellis Park, a stadium at which they have traditionally produced their best performances.

Still, South Africa had been a distant second in Sydney, where Wallaby flyhalf Stephen Larkham had delivered a masterful performance in putting them to the sword.

The Aussies were also keen to continue embarrassing White for a statement in the build-up to the Sydney game where he suggested that their loosehead prop, Bill Young, wouldn't be taken seriously if he rocked up to train at the University of Stellenbosch.

It was probably more a reference to Young's small frame than anything else, but the extremity of the statement suggested that it was intended as a little bit of psychological warfare.

Young's scrumming technique had always been considered illegal within South African ranks, but his team won the round in Sydney after he had responded to White's statement by saying that he would be scrumming against "dinosaurs".

The Wallabies' build-up for the return fixture in Johannesburg had been all but ideal.

They prepared in Cape Town, where reserve scrumhalf Matt Henjak, wings Lote Tuqiri and Wendell Sailor, and loosehead prop Matt Dunning had all breached team protocol when they went to a nightclub on the Thursday before the test.

The disciplinary process would only run its course the following week during the Aussies' preparation for the Tri-Nations match at Loftus in Pretoria. Henjak ended up being sent home, while the others got off lightly with fines.

But, while there were clearly disciplinary issues in the team, the Wallabies still looked a formidable side on paper. This was all the more so when White appeared to have selected a weakened side.

Having picked a large quotient of players of colour, the Springbok coach felt it necessary to have a talk with referee Steve Walsh beforehand.

"There had been a massive amount of media coverage about the nine players of colour and it being a transformed team," White recalls.

"When I went to Steve, I said, 'I just want to tell you one thing: just because there are more players of colour than usual, it doesn't mean we are weaker'. He said, 'No, I appreciate that'.

"I also said to him that if there were eight Maoris in the All Black team, people would assume that the team would be stronger. That wouldn't necessarily be the case because a team should be judged on its merits.

"I think that talk helped a lot because he wouldn't enter the game with pre-conceived ideas."

But South Africa's biggest ally was neither Ellis Park nor a chat with the referee. It was Madiba Magic.

An ageing Mandela was fieldside on a golf cart with wife Graça Machel before kick-off and Springbok captain John Smit was fully determined to use the great man's presence to the Boks' advantage.

"I drew inspiration from who he was, what he did and what he had gone through. I think most people do," says Smit.

"His presence lifted us. Here was Nelson Mandela taking out his Saturday to come and wish us luck. He took a massive amount of interest in Jake's team and had a huge influence. We were often invited to his residence and he knew the guys by name.

"When he came to a game he didn't simply make us realise how special the occasion was; it also had a huge effect on the opposition."

With that in mind, Smit spotted an opportunity.

"I asked Annelee Murray (the Springboks' Public Relations and Events Manager) to make sure that the Australians see Madiba in the tunnel when they return from their warm-up. They would have five or six minutes to think about what was happening," he recalls.

"And so Madiba was in a golf cart at the top of the tunnel and we had finished our warm-up before them. I noticed it and said, 'Madiba, thanks for coming' and started chatting to him.

"We gathered around him in his cart because he couldn't get to the change room. Annelee had brought us out early so what we could gather around him for a minute and a half.

"Here a Springbok team that had just completed its warm-up was gathered around a golf cart! We were seven minutes away from kick-off and every guy was hanging onto every word he was saying.

"It was almost poetry because the Aussies came behind us and had to squeeze past his buggy to get up to the stairs on the left. You could see they were star-struck. They were just put off-centre by the presence of this unbelievably great man, who is revered the world over as a god, let alone just a man.

"I believe his presence affected us positively and had the opposition thinking that a man of his incredible stature wanted us to win. They would think, 'It's almost bad of us to try and go against him!'"

White continues the story.

"I remember the Wallabies' eyes. They looked at him and thought 'oh geesh, him again' because they realised what a boost he would be to our players."

With Mandela's spell cast, the Boks set purposefully about demolishing the Wallabies.

As had been the case in several of the Springboks' victories under White, they were particularly clever in punching off the ropes.

Larkham, so influential in crafting South Africa's doom in Sydney, was largely at fault for conceding the first try. The Aussies attacked down the blind side and as he was stopped in his tracks, he tried to find his half-back partner George Gregan with a pass back. Jean de Villiers, playing at inside centre for the Boks after he had often been used as a wing in the early stages of White's tenure, intercepted and sprinted away for the try.

Fullback Percy Montgomery, who had earlier exchanged penalties with Wallaby inside centre Matt Giteau, converted and the Boks were up 10-3.

Montgomery added another penalty before another intercept took the Boks three scores away from the Wallabies. As with the first try, Australia attacked and this time it was outside centre Stirling Mortlock's pass aimed at left wing Lote Tuqiri that was pounced on by Bok flyhalf André Pretorius. He passed to left wing Bryan Habana, who finished next to the left upright. Montgomery added the conversion and the Boks were 20-3 up with only 21 minutes played.

But the Boks were knocked out of their stride by yellow cards to right wing Breyton Paulse and openside flank Schalk Burger either side of half-time.

Paulse got his marching orders in the 33rd minute for repeated infringements and the Wallabies managed to drive over for a try by No 8 David Lyons that reduced the deficit to 12 points.

But a long-range penalty by Montgomery shortly before half-time again put the Boks at least three scores ahead of the Wallabies.

Burger's yellow card two minutes into the second half – this time after he had accidentally struck Wallaby flank Rocky Elsom on the side of the face after flinging out an arm in desperate defence – further complicated South Africa's task.

The Boks were very briefly down to 13 men and their situation looked desperate as the Wallabies set up a lineout close to their try-line. But lock Victor Matfield grabbed Australian hooker Jeremy Paul's throw and the danger was averted.

Paulse then re-entered the fray and South Africa needed only 14 men to score their third and also the best try of the game. They struck off first phase, with De Villiers breaking the defensive line as he came on an angled run and collected the ball from Pretorius. Having beaten Wallaby scrum-half George Gregan, he slipped through two more Wallabies before finding centre partner Jaque Fourie on his outside with the scoring pass.

Montgomery converted and added another penalty to give the Boks a remarkable 33-8 lead with 23 minutes to go.

The platform was there to wipe the floor with a very good Wallaby side, but instead the visitors managed to bring a degree of respectability to the scoreboard.

Larkham and Paul scored tries in the 70th and 78th minutes respectively, but it was a lost cause.

White also used all three players of colour on his bench, with Julies replacing De Villiers, Shimange going on for Andrews, and Sephaka for Steenkamp.

It was a triumph for White and his Boks in more ways than one. Not only had they comprehensively outplayed the Wallabies, but they had done so with a 22-man squad that could even charm the Parliamentary Portfolio Committee on Sport.

"The nine players of colour was unheard of and wasn't done to make a statement. There was a genuine belief in those guys. I suppose it did end up making a statement," says Smit.

"Invariably the public would think 'here comes trouble' when a team like that is selected. It was a South African moment rather than a Springbok moment because it was probably something that was necessary.

"It is irrelevant that those nine guys were good enough to play for South Africa. It was necessary from a South African point of view to change the impression the masses had about the Springbok team.

"It was one of those moments that helped, like in 1995. Madiba was there, there were nine players of colour in the 22-man squad, and the Boks went on to beat great opposition by playing phenomenally well.

"That was a great moment for the squad, but probably more so for the country in my view. What did irritate me was that the focus became how many players of colour had played and not how well we played as a team.

"Jake deserved more credit because he believed in those guys. We were well coached, well drilled and knew what to do. But that was never going to be the story."

But boy, did the Boks play well.

"It was beautiful," says Smit.

"I was terrified before every test – even when we played Uruguay because you know that you are not allowed to lose those games. That terror leaves your body during the game when things go well.

"I just recall feeling that it would go well from the first to the 80th minute. And it did."

Looking back, White has the highest praise for the performance.

"That is the best we ever played. There is no doubt in my mind," he says.

"It was the coming together of how I wanted the team to play – on attack and defence. It was our best attacking performance. We played running rugby, asked questions of the Wallaby defence, stepped, off-loaded and made the right decisions."

Of the black players who started in Johannesburg, only Steenkamp, Habana and Paulse remained in the starting line-up for the opening Tri-Nations fixture against the same opposition in Pretoria the following Saturday. Sephaka, Januarie and Julies were on the bench.

Jones took heart from the fact that Mandela wouldn't be there for what would be the opening match of the Tri-Nations and even mentioned at a press conference that the Springboks would not be able to draw on the same extraordinary motivation.

As expected, Australia proved tougher opposition in Pretoria, with a converted try by flank George Smith in the 39th minute giving them a half-time lead of 13-6.

This time, however, it was South Africa that finished stronger.

It was a well-worked backline move off first phase that drew them level.

Scrumhalf Fourie du Preez passed the ball flat to De Villiers, who then found Pretorius behind him.

The flyhalf flung the ball out to the right, where Habana had popped up off his wing. Habana surged forward and, finding himself between defenders, off-loaded expertly to Mongomery, who in turn off-loaded to Paulse.

The diminutive right wing finished and celebrated his try with a trade-mark flick-flack.

Australia still managed a penalty that gave them a 16-13 lead with just 21 minutes left. But the Boks remained on top and Montgomery added two more penalties as the pressure on the Wallabies took its toll.

The second one, which gave them the lead for the first time since Montgomery had put them 3-0 up early in the game, came six minutes before the end.

It was a nail-biting finish, but Pretorius capped a composed Bok performance with a drop goal, which meant the Boks had outscored a very decent Wallaby side 16-3 in the second half to win 22-16.

As for the black players that so pleased the rugby fraternity on a wonderful day at Ellis Park, not all of their careers kicked on.

It was only Steenkamp's, Habana's, Paulse's, Januarie's and, to a lesser extent, Andrews' Springbok careers that wouldn't just peter out.

Tyibilika played four more tests – against Argentina in Buenos Aires later that year and another three in the 2006 Tri-Nations during Schalk Burger's injury-enforced absence.

Sephaka played five more tests and his Springbok career ended against Ireland in Dublin in November 2006. He had a spell with the Leopards before his rugby playing career ended at the Lions in 2010.

Julies only played four more tests, with his final appearance in the Boks' narrow escape in their World Cup match against Tonga in Lens in 2007.

Shimange played twice more, with White losing interest in his services after the victory over Scotland in Durban in June 2006.

Andrews gradually slipped out of favour and he ended as a substitute in both South Africa's Tri-Nations matches when they fielded weakened teams against the Wallabies in Sydney and the All Blacks in Christchurch in 2007.

Paulse also finished on that tour as his test career ran out of legs just before the World Cup in France.

Habana, Steenkamp and Januarie all went to the World Cup in 2007, though the latter was no longer a serious challenger for White's strongest line-up by then.

If only briefly, however, all nine played their part on a very significant day for Springbok rugby.

CHAPTER 13

Teetering on the Brink

"I threw the ball to André Pretorius and said, 'Petoors, eerder jy as ek'!"
– JOHN SMIT

The Springboks' ability to produce big victories with their backs to the wall should be the basis of a PhD thesis rather than a topic that continues to – and probably always will - fascinate sports writers.

It is how coach Jake White was saved on two occasions in a tumultuous 2006 in which South Africa sank as low as losing 0-49 to Australia in Brisbane. No Springbok team had sunk that low before.

Everything that possibly could go wrong did, including a serious neck injury to Schalk Burger in the wake of the second test against Scotland in Port Elizabeth. The outstanding flank was ruled out for the rest of the season – a development White said was akin to losing three players.

By the time the Springboks lined up for their home Tri-Nations match against the All Blacks at the Royal Bafokeng Sports Palace in Rustenburg on 2 September 2006, they had lost five tests on the trot.

The sequence started with a 26-36 defeat to France at Newlands before their Tri-Nations campaign kicked off with the embarrassing result in Brisbane. New Zealand then beat the Springboks 35-17 in Wellington and a second test against Australia in Sydney was lost 18-20.

There was no immediate respite on home soil and when the Springboks lost 26-45 to a below strength All Black side, White was desperately clinging to his job.

So who could foresee a 21-20 victory for South Africa in Rustenburg, especially as New Zealand coach Graham Henry picked what the media termed his "A team" for that test on 2 September 2006?

But, as the crisis grew, the South African Rugby Union (Saru) also called the "A team" by inviting a number of former Springbok coaches to a brainstorming session with the incumbent. White says he didn't learn anything new on the rugby front, but that the forum may have given his bosses some important food for thought.

"It helped in a sense because the former coaches said to Saru, 'Why are you lambasting the coach because nothing has changed? All the problems and concerns we had were exactly what Jake has raised.'

"There weren't pearls of wisdom that they gave me that made the team play better, but what it did was make Oregan Hoskins (Saru president) realise that maybe the problem wasn't always with the coach.

"Maybe the problem was sometimes with what happens around the structures. It gave me a massive amount of confidence that they had almost helped me by saying, 'Listen, it's no use trying to get rid of the coach. This time last year you said he was the best coach in the world. Now you want to fire him.'"

But the Springbok coach remained under a great deal of pressure going into the match in Rustenburg and general consensus was that he would face the sack if things went pear-shaped again.

In the days leading up to the test, White tried to hatch a plan to negate New Zealand's strength of their enormous, pacey and skilful outside backs.

"I remember getting to the field that week and seeing that it had been marked close to the athletics track. I thought what I'd try to do was find a way in which it could be narrowed," he recalls.

"I contacted André Watson (Saru's Referees Manager) and told him that I was very worried about the field. I was aware that, according to the laws of the game, there had to be some sort of action if you were concerned about something dangerous regarding the field.

"Their response was, 'Are you serious?' and I said, 'I'm dead serious'. I asked the groundsman whether he could move the lines inwards and he said that he couldn't because the field had already been marked. It's amazing because I thought they'd move heaven and earth to help us in our country."

"I remember that it was a big media issue about why I wanted to change the field. My approach was to ask who would be liable if there were injuries. It was a ploy. I thought I could neutralise New Zealand's pace by moving the field two metres in. They were going to run from side to side and defending would probably be a lot easier if the field was narrowed."

White says he had the backing of Watson and agreement by All Blacks coach Graham Henry, but meetings on the issue came to naught.

As it turned out, the pressure the Boks piled on the All Blacks made it impossible for the visitors to play to their strengths in any event.

Flyhalf André Pretorius, lock Victor Matfield and flank Pierre Spies, in particular, played very well, but All Black No 8 Rodney So'oialo had such a nightmare that he was comfortably South Africa's best player.

He gifted South Africa their first try with a suicidal pass, which was intercepted by speedster Bryan Habana for a converted try that gave the Springboks a 13-10 lead.

New Zealand then had a try by Andrew Hore disallowed after So'oialo had illegally taken out Springbok centre Jean de Villiers to pave the way for his hooker.

But All Black flyhalf Dan Carter added another penalty and the match was delicately poised at 13-all at half-time.

South Africa were first on the board in the second half, with No 8 Pedrie Wannenburg finishing in the 55th minute after a good attacking spell.

The All Blacks then edged into a 20-18 lead in the 66th minute with a converted try by right wing Joe Rokocoko after a cross-kick by outside centre Mils Muliaina.

But So'oialo paved the way for a Springbok victory by foolishly storming in from the side at a ruck. It was probably down to frustration more than anything else because he took Matfield out in the process. The Springbok lock had produced another dominant display and made the All Blacks' lives particularly difficult.

Pretorius held his nerve to slot the penalty three minutes before the end and the Boks won 21-20.

"Rodney helped us. He had a nightmare," White recalls with a smile.

The Springboks followed that up with a convincing 24-16 win over Australia in Johannesburg and the two consecutive victories were enough to save White from the sack.

He is convinced it would have been the end had they lost in Rustenburg.

"The pressure was unbelievable. That was probably the defining moment in my coaching career because if we had lost I'm almost sure that they would have paid me out and got rid of me. We then followed it up with the win over Australia in which JP Pietersen played his first test."

White believes that injuries to Burger and lock Bakkies Botha, together with the tough schedule, made 2006 a very difficult year.

One of the problems the coach had that year was the impact of injuries to the likes of Burger and Botha on a defensive system rated the best in the world a few seasons previously.

"We had what we called a 'washing machine' defensive system. What it meant was that we chased opponents to certain positions and then we'd defend them there. A lot of people said it wasn't working anymore, but I didn't have the same personnel. I had to coach the new guys to have the same skills set," says White.

"It wasn't a problem for Schalk and Bakkies to defend in the middle of the field because they could tackle efficiently in that area. When you have a lock who had previously played flank like Bakkies and a great defender like Schalk next to one another, it's very different to having new boys who don't necessarily defend the same way.

"One of the things I said to myself before we got to that test is that I needed a way to get the new players to learn the skill and not change the system. I knew that if I changed it, we would find it hard to go back to what was working for us.

"I remember we brought in AJ Venter and Pedrie Wannenburg (both loose forwards) for that test. We were quite fortunate that they were fit and available. They could just about do the same things as the players I was missing.

"It doesn't excuse us being poor, but 2006 was the third year of a cycle and then you are always going to have to bring something new to the table.

"I don't know where the 49-0 defeat to Australia came from. To this day it's a freak thing because we were never as poor as 49-0. It was one of those games where we dug ourselves into a hole. We should have beaten Australia in Sydney after that.

"We just got into a downward spiral and, no matter who you are as a player or coach, once you lose confidence you start doubting whether you are doing the right thing."

John Smit, who led the Springboks into battle in Rustenburg, reckons it was a "watershed" victory.

"We had to win that test because we were five down on the trot. I could have kissed So'oialo on the lips when he came in from the side at that ruck! It was an absolute brain fart," Smit recalls.

"It was our last chance. I threw the ball to André Pretorius and said, 'Petoors, eerder jy as ek!' He just smiled at me and I thought to myself that the one thing he could do was kick under pressure."

As Smit thought would be the case, Pretorius held his nerve to arrest a downward spiral that was threatening to derail White's coaching career.

"When you get into a run like that it's very difficult to just turn things around. You need anything just to get a result. You become desperate and it becomes harder," says Smit.

"You're caught in a downward spiral and then you have to face the All Blacks. We needed that game and it was the old case of the Springboks being cornered. We were desperate."

The high stakes resulted in an ill-tempered match.

"There was nothing pretty about that test. All tests are physical, but there was a lot of niggle, fighting and punching," Smit recalls.

"I still remember Jerry Collins (All Black flank) coming to me afterwards and saying, 'Smittie, we play hard, but we don't do that' because both teams were guilty. It was just a result of what that test meant.

"The good tests between the All Blacks and Springboks aren't dirty. They are simply won by big hits and physicality."

So White lived to fight another day, little knowing that that day was just around the corner.

With the World Cup a year away, White followed the advice of leading sports scientist Tim Noakes to rest a handful of key Springboks for the end-of-season tour in 2006.

Lock Victor Matfield, scrumhalf Fourie du Preez, loosehead prop Os du Randt and fullback Percy Montgomery were all rested in a bid to have them fresh come the 2007 showpiece in France.

The intention was also to rest wing Bryan Habana, but an injury to Jaque Fourie necessitated his involvement.

White also had to continue to make do without Burger and Botha.

The aim of the tour was partly to blood some new talent, with Bevin Fortuin starting at fullback, and Frans Steyn and Jaco Pretorius on the wings, in the opening test against Ireland in Dublin.

Jaco Pretorius, of course, was a specialist outside centre, but the No 13 jersey was handed to Habana – presumably because the defensive and organisational demands of the position are best served by an experienced player.

The circumstances meant that Smit also led into battle a team in which he, Spies, De Villiers and André Pretorius were the only remaining players in the starting line-up from the last test against Australia in Johannesburg.

Little wonder then that the match against Ireland proved a disaster, with the Springbok's defence badly exposed in a 15-32 defeat. Ireland had led 22-3 at half-time.

England then loomed large on the horizon, with both White and opposing coach Andy Robinson's positions looking precarious.

White's team should have comfortably won the first test after taking an 18-6 lead early in the second half courtesy of right wing Akona Ndungane's try. However, England clawed their way back and clinched the game after tighthead prop Phil Vickery scored from a ruck close to the Springboks' try-line.

"I thought we should have won the first test. We let it slip, so much so that the players said, 'Thank goodness we have them next week because we can actually beat these guys'," White recalls.

If White's job wasn't on the line before he toured, it certainly was as the Boks approached the second test against England on 25 November 2006.

They would also play a tour match against a World XV in Leicester the following weekend and White had word that he would have to return home before that game to explain himself to Saru's Presidents Council. This followed a motion of no confidence in him by the Blue Bulls Rugby Union.

But in the meantime there was the more pressing matter of having to beat England. They knew that it was within their grasp.

South Africa and White's position nevertheless looked dire as England built a 14-3 lead after half an hour.

But the response was superb: André Pretorius added two penalties to his earlier drop goal and then loosehead prop CJ van der Linde finished for a converted try before half-time.

It gave the Boks a morale-boosting 16-14 lead before a controlled second half performance in which André Pretorius did a "Jannie" by adding three more drop goals to finish with an extraordinary tally of four in a 25-14 win.

Pretorius finished the game one drop goal shy of Jannie de Beer's record five against England in the World Cup quarter-final of 1999.

White remains aghast at the events that followed the second test against England.

"One of the toughest things in my career was telling the players that I was leaving (to face the Presidents Council). Frans Steyn, who was a young guy and had lived his entire life to become a Springbok, came to me and asked, 'Are you coming back?'", the coach recalls.

"I don't know how to put it in words, but the impression in my mind was, 'What a cocked up environment we have in South African rugby. We try to get these boys to make representing the Springboks the epitome of their careers and then we literally fly the coach home. And you have to tell a young boy of 19 that.'

"We take it for granted: he becomes a Springbok, gets his blazer and understands things. But that is not the real world. The real world is that the All Black coach doesn't get summonsed home."

Sensing that White's head could potentially roll, Noakes – a key ally who was consulted on day one by the coach regarding the long-term conditioning of players – wrote to Hoskins the day before the second test against England.

In his letter, Noakes pleaded White's case, stating that the coach had been advised by him and the team's medical support staff to rest key players so that they would be fit for the World Cup the following year.

It was a brave decision by the coach, who Noakes said had put his job at risk by resting players in the best interests of South African rugby.

Noakes' letter may well have helped White see off the vote of no confidence.

Saru's meeting was held at the Holiday Inn Garden Court in Woodstock near Cape Town's city centre and journalists camped outside the room where White was explaining himself to the blazer brigade.

The coach then had to leave the room before the voting and common sense prevailed as the delegates decided by 15 votes to four to retain his services.

However absurd the notion that a Springbok coach should return home during a tour, the entire episode had a positive spin-off as it brought certainty that White would lead the Springboks to the World Cup the following year.

Furthermore, he had taken a big step towards a successful World Cup by resting key players.

"If you recall I got sign-off from the Presidents Council that I was allowed to take a young team. Had I known my job was on the line and it was a matter of do or die, I would have picked all the top players," says White.

"The resting of the players was a scientific recommendation by Professor Noakes. He saved my job by informing Saru that he had advised me to rest key players for South Africa to be able to win the World Cup. They would break down if they weren't rested.

"I knew the franchises wouldn't rest the players in Super Rugby. The only time I could rest them (before the World Cup year) was in 2006."

White thought the line of questioning in the meeting to be absurd.

"One of the questions at the meeting was, 'Is John Smit the right captain?'

The one guy said he went to a lot of bars and restaurants and people tell him that John isn't the right captain. I don't understand how John can then achieve such extraordinary success as a captain.

"Some of the questions were, 'Why do I play Frans Steyn and Jaco Pretorius on the wing?', and, 'Why do I play Bryan Habana at centre?' Those are things I tried out on that tour.

"I look back at that test against England and think back on that period as the most trying time in my career as an international coach. I knew then they were trying to find whatever they could to nail me."

White actually had a glance of the voting inside as he stood outside with a couple of the presidents who didn't want to vote.

"The door swung open as someone went inside and I saw some with their hands up. I can't recall who and don't know what the hands up or down meant.

"But the irony, which is incredible, is that after we won the World Cup each one of them had his arm around me at a banquet and said he didn't think I should go.

"None of them said he'll put his hand up and apologise. Everyone to a man said he was one of the guys who said I should stay. That meant I would have had a full house of votes, which I know I didn't."

But sanity had at least prevailed towards the end of 2006. White had survived and amidst all the tumult managed to rest key players. A 19-year-old Frans Steyn had also stepped confidently into the test arena.

And now, with the benefit of that most perfect science called hindsight, we can say that there were some crucial seeds sown for World Cup glory.

Playing a 59

*"Throughout that four-year period, Jake continuously spoke of producing
the equivalent of a round of 59 in golf on the rugby field."*
– BRYAN HABANA

There will always be more highlights on the horizon for Springbok rugby,
but South Africa's 36-0 victory over England in a World Cup pool match
in Paris on 14 September 2007 will not easily lose its status as one of the
biggest.

It was as complete a performance as the Springboks had delivered in
the post-isolation phase and a case of reaping what coach Jake White had
been sowing since 2004. White's master plan eventually culminated in captain John Smit lifting the Webb Ellis Cup after South Africa had beaten the
same opponents 15-6 in the final at the same venue on 20 October 2007.

It started as soon as White selected a team to play Ireland in his first
match in charge in Bloemfontein in 2004. There were five forwards – Smit
(hooker), Os du Randt (loosehead prop), Bakkies Botha, Victor Matfield
(both locks) and Schalk Burger (flank) – that would start in the final.
Fourie du Preez, who would over time become the world's best scrumhalf, was also there.

White added the other pieces of the puzzle along the way, discarded
a few on their merits along with those handed to him against his will,
came through numerous skirmishes, and clung on desperately throughout the journey. But ultimately he had the resolve to stick to his plan and
make the brave calls that would result in glory.

Many of South Africa's rugby bosses were happy to see the back of White when his tenure ended, but they will never able to dispute his contribution to the game and his country.

And the 36-0 victory in a decisive Pool A match is certainly one he will always be able to dine out on.

But it was not simply one of those days where the Springboks could seemingly do no wrong and where the ball bounced in their favour. The standard of their performance had a lot to do with the building blocks, in particular the strategic rest for top players and a smart build-up to the tournament.

White left Matfield, Du Preez, Du Randt and fullback Percy Montgomery behind for the Springboks' end-of-season tour in 2006. A second-string side was also sent to tour Australia and New Zealand in the 2007 Tri-Nations.

Both decisions obviously resulted in adverse results with the exception being the last test of 2006 against England at Twickenham. Had it not been for that victory of 25-14, the strategy to rest players would probably have cost White his job. The second string sides that were fielded in the Tri-Nations also triggered an inter-continental tiff with Sanzar partners Australia and New Zealand.

But White was able to soldier on and the warm-up games for the World Cup were handpicked to ensure optimal performance come the first pool match against Samoa.

South Africa would play Namibia at Newlands and then go on tour for matches against Irish side Connacht and Scotland.

White says he had to fight for those fixtures as Saru had made promises to other unions in an effort to secure the hosting of the 2011 World Cup. New Zealand were confirmed as hosts in November 2005 after winning the bidding war against South Africa and Japan.

"I got a lot of calls from people about who we should be playing in the friendlies prior to the World Cup. There were promises made by Saru to other unions about friendlies if they voted for us, not thinking that maybe the coach feels we shouldn't be playing against those countries," he says.

"So there was a lot of animosity between myself and Saru leading up to the World Cup because I said, 'I'm not playing those guys'. Their view was that we needed to do what was necessary for the bid to be successful.

"I could see what was happening with all the promises. As it subsequently happened, some of those countries didn't vote for us. I then got the message not to worry because we wouldn't be playing them. And I said I was never going to play them anyway.

"The reason I'm telling that story is that it was no coincidence that we played Namibia, Connacht and Scotland. Those were the ones I decided on. The success in the pool match against England had its roots in what we did in the run-up to the tournament. Some of the other teams played stupid trial games.

"We knew that the pool match against England would be our fifth in a sequence of matches that started with the warm-up games and tapered it like that. Namibia was an easy game at home and then the game against Connacht would be for the guys who wouldn't be in our first-choice line-up at the World Cup. It gave me insight into what they would be like as a group.

"The game against Scotland was our last run-out against an international side before we played in the World Cup. I knew that if we played well there, we'd take that confidence into the tournament.

"After that we'd have our opening match against Samoa, who were ranked lower than England. The match against England would then be our benchmark of where we were as a side.

"So it wasn't just about winning 36-0. It was how the jigsaw puzzle had come together in the weeks leading up to that. We had progressed from thrashing Namibia to beating England 36-0.

"It was massive. Not so much from a results point of view as the confidence it engendered. Having beaten England 36-0, we knew we could win the World Cup."

Getting there had also involved discipline and sacrifices from the players. Up until that point in the tournament, they had not allowed themselves alcohol or the presence of wives and girlfriends.

"We felt those were the kind of sacrifices we would have to make," says White.

"There would be no going out, no partying, no wives or girlfriends or whatever. The reason I'm placing that in the context is that we always knew the games against Samoa and England would be a benchmark for where we ended in the World Cup."

Much as was the case in 1995, a lot would depend on how the team handled the inevitable headwinds on their journey.

It didn't take long for something akin to the Black South-Easter to swirl through the camp – in the aftermath of the Springboks' 59-7 win over Samoa in their opening game at the Parc des Princes.

Centre Jean de Villiers, who had started as a wing under White in 2004 and had progressed steadily to become a mainstay and establish himself as arguably the leading No 12 in the world, tore a bicep early in the second half.

Then, in the aftermath, flank Schalk Burger was cited for allegedly tackling Samoan scrumhalf Junior Polu in the air. Burger was suspended for four games – something White likened to the tournament basically losing its Diego Maradona – but mercifully the ban was reduced to two matches on appeal.

As it turned out, De Villiers' injury became an entry point for Frans Steyn to stamp down his considerable authority on the tournament, while Wikus van Heerden did a fabulous stand-in job for Burger against the English.

Steyn himself was later cited for allegedly biting Tongan wing Joseph Vaka in South Africa's third pool match in Lens, but the case was dismissed.

Captain John Smit says the team's positive mental state, which had been moulded in the three-and-a-half seasons preceding the 2007 showpiece, meant that any blow could be absorbed.

"I put my arm around Jean as I walked into the dressing room after the Samoa game and he was crying because he knew it was over. That was a difficult moment. I think everyone went to him, and felt and saw his pain," Smit recalls.

"As a group we were emotionally and spiritually connected, so things like that drew us closer together. We realised that this guy had made the journey for three and a half years and couldn't follow through on it. It made what we were doing that much more important. The approach was that, no matter what was thrown at us, we would simply adjust out of respect for one another and what had been done in those preceding three and a half years.

"Wikus was tough as nails and a great guy. That is something people often miss about successful teams – you sometimes get a group that are good people let alone good rugby players. They connect on a level outside of rugby and that is what we had. Wikus was one of those good people who had a huge amount of courage.

"The attitude we had as a team meant that we saw Frans coming in for Jean as an opportunity. We just thought that we now had a guy in the team who could kick the ball a mile and this was an opportunity to use him. I believe the attitude of the people around him helped Frans to have a good World Cup. "Every challenge we faced almost made us stronger as we gathered this collective momentum along the journey."

Smit puts that steely resolve and the team's supreme confidence down to White's astute management from 2004 onwards.

"The team just had this amazing ability to stay calm and believe. That was a by-product of what was coached and taught by Jake. So every obstacle, yellow card and citing was more fuel to the fire.

"If I look back now, you could see the steeliness in every single guy's eyes when we walked out of the tunnel. Each one of them knew what he wanted and what needed to be done to achieve the goal. That is what 36-0 was. Every guy was on the same page and wanted the same thing."

Left wing Bryan Habana, who would end up being named the International Rugby Board's Player of the Year after a tournament in which he scored eight tries, highlights the fact that the performance was a result of a process that had started well before the World Cup.

"We had been building up to that game against England because we knew that a victory would give us an easier route to the final. Throughout that four-year period, Jake continuously spoke of producing the equivalent of a round of 59 in golf on the rugby field," Habana recalls.

"We had put a lot of hard work and effort into making sure that we would achieve what we ultimately did. Jake constantly emphasised the importance of that England game.

"We weren't tackling tackle bags with England jumpers on. It was just a mental preparation. We knew how important the game was. We were unbelievably professional in how we went about things.

"It was a fantastic experience and great to be part of. If ever I experienced a complete performance, that was it. Everything just worked for us. It was one of the best games I have been involved in.

"Fourie du Preez had one of the best games I have ever seen a scrumhalf play – not just in the Springbok jumper but in any team in the world. He laid a platform and was unbelievable. He played guys into gaps. His communication, execution and decision-making were world class.

"Percy Montgomery's kicking was flawless, while JP Pietersen achieved something phenomenal by scoring two tries as a 21-year-old. The platform laid by the forwards was amazing and Juan Smith murdered the England pack with his presence.

"It was a fantastic game from which we gained a lot of motivation and belief."

If the Springboks played a 59, the English were out of bounds. They were unable to muster a reply to anything that the Springboks threw at them.

The fact that the defending champions ultimately made it as far as the final is just another pointer to those remarkable twists and turns that World Cup tournaments tend to take.

Having achieved their defining moment against the English, the Springboks were finally allowed the company of wives and girlfriends. And, of course, to have a few drinks.

White immediately picked his team for the match against Tonga in Lens and his troops knew in advance who would play. He was going to give his so-called "B-team" a run.

As it turned out, the Félix-Bollaert Stadium very nearly proved the scene of one of the biggest upsets in World Cup history. South Africa's second string only led 7-3 at half-time and in the 44th minute fell behind to Tongan tighthead prop Kisi Pulu's converted try.

White had seen enough and called on the men he would have preferred to have kept wrapped in cotton wool. Smit, Steyn, Habana, Smith, lock Victor Matfield and tighthead prop BJ Botha were all sent on to effect a turnaround.

Flyhalf André Pretorius, who had missed four penalties, was also put out of his misery close to the hour mark with the introduction of Montgomery.

But the Springboks could easily have lost had the ball bounced unfavourably in the dying embers. Tongan flyhalf Pierre Hola kicked the ball down into the right-hand corner, but mercifully it rolled into touch rather than sit up for Tongan wing Tevita Hemilitoni Tu'ifua. The Springboks scraped home by 30-25.

A defeat would not have changed the pool standings, but White believes it could have been disastrous in the overall scheme of things.

"The momentum you get from one game to the next is the spur to winning the World Cup," he says.

"It's not just about confidence, but also about what match officials think. If you're bad enough to lose a game like that, they don't see you as a strong enough force to win the World Cup."

The positive spin-off from an awful performance for White was that he would no longer have to explain selections to his players going forward.

"The difference between our A and B sides was massive. Selection after the match against Tonga was never going to be a problem because there was no discussion. My selection meetings never had to take long because players couldn't knock on my door and ask what more they needed to do to be picked," says White.

"They all got a chance and were measured at the same World Cup."

The Boks brought back their heavyweights for the pool match against the USA at the Stade de la Mosson in Montpellier, but a runaway victory of 64-15 was soured by a tournament-ending knee injury to tighthead prop BJ Botha.

Next up was a quarter-final against Fiji at the Stade Vélodrome in Marseille.

It was a weekend on which the tournament exploded into life, with the biggest shock in Cardiff where favourites New Zealand were controversially beaten 20-18 by France, sparking wild celebrations in the host country.

England had also managed a remarkable turnaround by scrumming

Bryan Habana equalled Jonah Lomu's record of eight tries at a World Cup in 2007 and would later become South Africa's all-time leading try-scorer.

A picture that perhaps captures former president Nelson Mandela's influence on South African rugby.

Top: Captain John Smit and coach Jake White show off the Webb Ellis Cup after the 15-6 victory over England in the World Cup final of 2007.

Above left: André Pretorius perhaps played an important part in South African rugby history by rescuing coach Jake White from the sack with his boot in 2006.

Above right: Jake White with legendary loosehead prop Os du Randt, who would be integral to his coach's plans from 2004 until the World Cup final in 2007.

Ricky Januarie is congratulated by team-mates Bryan Habana and Juan Smith after scoring the winning try in the 30-28 victory over New Zealand at Carisbrook in 2008.

While he was a controversial appointment in 2008, Peter de Villiers enjoyed some significant highs as Springbok coach

Above: Bakkies Botha was the enforcer in the Springbok pack during his glittering career.

Regs. Jaque Fourie on his way to scoring a magnificent try in the record 42-6 thumping of England at Twicken-ham in 2008.

Opposite top: Springbok loosehead prop Tendai Mtawarira squares up to British and Irish Lions tighthead Phil Vickery at a scrum. Mtawarira's annihilation of Vickery in the scrums during the first test at Kings Park in 2009 was decisive in securing South Africa's 26-21 victory.

Above left: Morné Steyn launches the last-gasp penalty that secured South Africa's series victory over the Lions at Loftus in 2009. The Springboks won the second test 28-25.

Above right: Steyn is congratulated by Andries Bekker.

Above: Frans Steyn kicks one of his three long-range penalties that helped South Africa secure the Tri-Nations crown in 2009 with a 32-29 victory over the All Blacks at the Waikato Stadium in Hamilton.

Right: Francois Louw lines up the NFL-style pass with which he set up Bryan Habana for his third try in the 31-8 victory over Australia at Loftus in 2012. Louw's impressive per-formances as openside

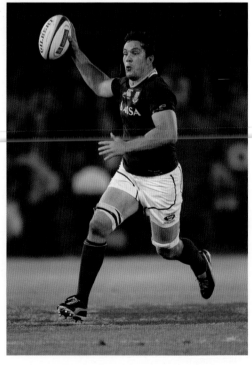

flank were among the highlights as the Springboks took tentative steps forward in Heyneke Meyer's first year as coach. *(Photograph by Christiaan Kotze, Foto24)*

Australia into submission and grinding out a 12-10 victory in the Stade
Vélodrome the day before South Africa were scheduled to play Fiji there.

And, for a while, it looked as if the Springboks might join the All Blacks
and Wallabies on the scrapheap.

The scoreline of 37-20 suggests that Fiji were beaten comfortably enough,
but who knows what might have been had it not been for a try-saving
tackle by Pietersen on lock Ifereimi Rawaqa in the final quarter.

South Africa were 23-20 up at the time and had lost their grip on a
game they had earlier led 20-6.

But with Pietersen's heroics serving as a spur, they regained their composure and a fruitful last 10 minutes produced tries for flank Juan Smith
and flyhalf Butch James.

With Argentina having beaten Scotland 19-13 in their quarter-final, the
Springboks had the scent of glory in their nostrils.

The Pumas were modest semi-final opposition and South Africa advanced to the final thanks to a comfortable 37-13 victory, with Habana's
brace of tries seeing him equal former All Black wing Jonah Lomu's record of eight in a tournament set in 1995.

A resurgent England then beat hosts France 14-9 to set up the unlikeliest of finals at the Stade de France.

Of course, not many people would have anticipated a final between
South Africa and England. The general expectation was that at least one
of the All Blacks, Wallabies and France would have been there.

With their exploits earlier in the tournament still fresh in the memory,
South Africa were rightly considered overwhelming favourites. But the
important thing was not to fall into the mental trap of believing their
publicity.

"The talk that whole week was that we would have to forget the 36-0
quickly because England had several World Cup winners in their side,"
says Habana.

"We also knew that the 36-0 victory had been achieved against a side with a number of injuries. Jonny Wilkinson (the famous English flyhalf) hadn't played. "But we still had our belief and, after watching New Zealand and Australia getting knocked out, we felt that we could really go on and win it."

White was not even willing to entertain the thought that the Springboks were favourites to dethrone England.

"Everyone thought it was a *fait accompli* that we were going to win because we had pumped England in the pool game. But when we stood in the change room we realised that one wall away there were several guys in the England squad who had won the World Cup in 2003.

"When you put things in perspective, you realise that we were not the favourites. We knew that part of our problem was that everyone expected us just to run out and win it without any fuss."

The players in the England squad who were also in their 22 for the World Cup final of 2003 were Wilkinson (flyhalf), Phil Vickery (tighthead prop), Ben Kay (lock), Martin Corry, Lewis Moody, Lawrence Dallaglio (all loose forwards), Mike Catt (inside centre) and Jason Robinson (fullback).

White credits veteran loosehead prop Os du Randt, who was in South Africa's World Cup-winning side of 1995, with a big role in calming the nerves.

"It dawned on the players in those last 15 minutes in the dressing room that we were 80 minutes away from something we may never get the opportunity to do again," says White.

"I think the younger guys then looked at Os and realised that he had actually won it before. It helped that we had spoken for such a long time about what Os had achieved."

Smit highlighted Du Randt's role from day one against Ireland in 2004.

"Os was an inspiration throughout the journey," he says.

"We could see how that guy struggled through the weeks with his knees – he was always in pain, training was hard for him and fitness was a nightmare. But he'd get through it.

"He was a father figure to all of us. There was definitely also a feeling that we were playing for Os. Every single guy in that change room while togging up looked to the corner where No 1 was – to look at Os and see how his eyes were and see what his body language was saying."

Smit points to a quiet confidence among the Springboks, even though they realised they were coming up against a very different English side in mentality and organisation to the one they had played against in their pool match.

"England had miraculously resurrected their campaign and you could see that the players had gone over the head of their coach (Brian Ashton), set him aside and said, 'We'll do this our way'. It worked and with that comes a belief," says Smit.

"We were playing a different England side, but we still believed that we had more than enough to deal with them."

The Springboks ended up being largely untroubled on their way to the 15-6 victory, with the only flutter of nerves coming early in the second half when England left wing Mark Cueto was over in the corner.

But television match official Stuart Dickinson – ironically a much-maligned figure in South Africa – made a marginal call in the Springboks' favour. Cueto had been forced out thanks to a last-gasp intervention by South African No 8 Danie Rossouw. A converted try would have given England a lead of 10-9.

Other than that it was a dull affair in which South Africa held an edge throughout, with their five penalties – four by Montgomery and one by Steyn – to Wilkinson's two underlining the difference.

Matfield was supreme in the lineouts, which meant England were limited in their ability to use the set-piece as an attacking platform.

The moment that effectively secured the victory was Steyn's long-range penalty of 46 metres in the 63rd minute. It gave the Springboks their decisive nine-point lead and took them out of danger of being hauled in via a converted try.

"As we got the penalty, I thought that Monty didn't have the distance in him," recalls Smit.

"I looked back and was looking for Frans, but couldn't find him because he was already walking towards the penalty spot. I thought, 'This *laaitie* wants to have a go. No problem. If he missed we'd be in England's 22-metre area in any event. If it went over, we'd be eight-plus points ahead.'

"When that kick went over I knew we'd win. England didn't have enough to breach us."

In fact, Smit does not believe it would have made a difference had Dickinson earlier ruled in Cueto's favour.

"The try would have swung the game, but it would have taken us out of third gear," he says.

"We would have done what was necessary. That is the zone we were in at that stage of the World Cup. It would have stopped us from being so conservative and calculated in the final."

But the mixture of composure and conservatism proved more than enough.

"When I saw John lift that trophy it wasn't a sure case of excitement and enjoyment. It was just relief," recalls Habana.

"There had been four years of toil, graft, ups and downs, highs and lows, good and bad times. This was the culmination of everything you had worked towards.

"There are specific moments in the game that you remember. You try and take in as much as possible. When you look back now . . . it's gone in the blink of an eye.

"To have achieved that with some phenomenal players but even more so with amazing friends was truly special and something I will treasure for the rest of my life."

CHAPTER 15

Storming the House of Pain

*"Are we going to be like other World Cup teams that go
through the motions and don't achieve anything more? Or are we
actually going to shut everyone up by pitching physically and
showing that we have the ability to beat the All Blacks?"*
— BAKKIES BOTHA

It's in the nature of sport to create myths and a prominent one in the minds of South Africans was the aura of Carisbrook.

The stadium's nickname – the House of Pain – together with the Springboks' inability to achieve success there until the 30-28 victory on 12 July 2008 – became imprinted in our minds and initially for no good reason.

Carisbrook only earned the nickname in 1992 when the coach of North Harbour at the time, Brad Meurant, baptised it as such at a post-match function after his side had lost to Otago in a semi-final of New Zealand's National Provincial Championship.

Meurant, by the way, actually has a South African connection – he was appointed as coach of Border in 1995.

By the time he made his pronouncement in 1992, which was reported by the *Otago Daily Times*, South Africa had only played there and lost three times – in 1921, 1956 and 1965.

Furthermore, the stadium itself was an old dog and with good reason pensioned off in favour of a new indoor facility for the 2011 Rugby World Cup.

However, South Africa continued to lose there in the post-isolation phase and as a result the nickname gained credence. There were four more defeats – in 1994, 1999, 2003 and 2005 before the flow was arrested.

Apart from the 11-19 loss in 2003 when no-one expected South Africa to win, the other three were significant.

The Springboks should on the balance of play have won instead of losing 14-22 in 1994. It wasn't a particularly strong All Black team against which they played and the defeat was a big psychological blow with two more tests to come. New Zealand clinched the series with a 13-9 victory in Wellington and it was honours even at 18-18 in the third test in Auckland.

The 0-28 defeat at Carisbrook in 1999 was a record at the time and an absolute humiliation for the Springboks, while the heartbreaking 27-31 loss in 2005 cost them the Tri-Nations title.

South Africa still headed the points table after the latter match, but New Zealand clinched the tournament a week later with a 34-24 win over Australia in Auckland.

So by the time 2008 came around the nickname was pretty apt, even though it had become an unhealthy South African obsession that militated against success because of the mental barrier it created.

And when a Springbok side coached by Peter de Villiers arrived there that year, the smart money was again on the All Blacks.

De Villiers had inherited a World Cup-winning side from Jake White, but the media and arguably the majority of supporters doubted his ability to build on that success after a committee appointed him Springbok coach ahead of the vastly more experienced Heyneke Meyer.

It is commonly held that there had been political interference to get De Villiers appointed.

South African Rugby Union (Saru) president Oregan Hoskins also said on the day of De Villiers's appointment that the issue of transformation had been taken seriously in arriving at the decision.

Opinion ended up being divided on De Villiers, whose inexperience showed as he struggled at press conferences and made numerous verbal gaffes.

But ultimately he captured the hearts of South Africans, who took a sympathetic view after the Springboks bowed out of the 2011 World Cup due to an inept refereeing performance by New Zealander Bryce Lawrence in their quarter-final against Australia.

The 2008 Tri-Nations came onto the horizon after a soft introduction to De Villiers's tenure with a two-match series against Wales, and a one-off test against Italy.

South Africa would not even begin to contemplate defeat against such opponents on home soil, but playing the All Blacks in New Zealand is rugby's ultimate challenge.

It would be accentuated by the fact that the Springboks would play the All Blacks on successive weekends – first in Wellington and then in Dunedin.

But for a terrific try finished off by left wing Bryan Habana shortly before half-time, the 8-19 defeat in Wellington did little to inspire confidence. South Africa also lost captain John Smit early in the match after he was dumped on his back by All Black lock Brad Thorn.

So it was with a bloodied nose and sans their first-choice captain that the Springboks had to march on.

But rather than retreating into their shells, they went on the offensive early in the week ahead of the clash in Carisbrook. Smit arrived to vent his fury over the incident that ended his tournament and for which Thorn had only been suspended for a week.

De Villiers also provided an unforgettable line in the press conference reported by *Die Burger*. When asked about the Springboks allegedly targeting star All Black flyhalf Dan Carter with late tackles, he offered this as part of his answer: "If you want to run with the big dogs then sometimes you have to lift your leg."

Presumably the old saying of, 'If you're gonna run with the big dogs, you can't pee like a puppy' got jumbled. But apart from entertaining,

De Villiers also upped the ante by stating that the All Blacks' scrumming was illegal.

New Zealand coach Graham Henry gave only a measured reply, but the Kiwi journalists did the talking on the All Blacks' behalf after their team had been picked for the test in Dunedin.

Jim Kayes wrote in the *Dominion Post* that the All Blacks' decision to rest tighthead prop Greg Somerville for the showdown in Dunedin was an indication that the once mighty Springbok scrum was no longer highly-rated.

And, of course, there was the rather predictable line from Wynne Gray in the *New Zealand Herald* questioning South Africa's status as world champions.

De Villiers also came under personal criticism, with the *Herald's* website attacking his selections in an article headlined "Wrong squad, wrong team – and wrong coach?"

But the worst was a comment by former All Black prop Craig Dowd dismissing De Villiers's claim about illegal scrumming and questioning his suitability for his position.

Newstalkzb.co.nz reported Dowd as saying that if De Villiers knew anything about rugby, he still had to see it. He believed there were good people on De Villiers's management team, but that the head coach was a "puppet".

Saru were infuriated by the remark and the chairman of SA Rugby (Pty) Ltd., Mpumelelo Tshume, demanded a public apology.

De Villiers then elevated the fight to a much higher level after the Springboks had more appropriately been welcomed with a guard of honour at Dunedin's airport upon arrival later in the week.

"It's quite stupid to say something like that. I don't know what his agenda is and whether it's maybe racism or not. Racism is a big issue in South Africa, but here [in New Zealand] and Australia as well," the Springbok coach said.

Dowd's response to *Die Burger* was that it was "pathetic" and "petty" to accuse him of racism, saying that his own comments should be seen in the context of De Villiers's role-playing at a press conference.

"Peter himself wouldn't know anything about scrumming. It should be seen within the context of the interview. It was definitely not my intention to run Peter down," he said.

But the battle lines had been drawn ahead of a test the Boks were widely expected to lose.

Lock Victor Matfield had to captain the side in Smit's absence, with Bismarck du Plessis filling the void at hooker and JP Pietersen coming in for Odwa Ndungane on the right wing.

But those weren't changes that would suddenly create the impression that South Africa could win at the House of Pain.

"We trained pretty well, but there was a real sense from outside the camp that we were beaten even before we started the game," recalls Springbok forwards coach Gary Gold.

"We heard from family back home that the sentiment was poor and that we apparently didn't stand a chance.

"We played on that from a coaching point of view because we believed that physically we could match the All Blacks. It was going to come down to work rate. We were quite critical of the players' performance on that front in Wellington.

"They hadn't worked hard enough off the ball, which you need to do against the All Blacks because of the width in their game."

A significant development in the week was a forwards meeting that Gold facilitated in the team hotel.

"We touched a little bit on why they had won the World Cup and that it was time to take it to the next level," recalls Gold.

"I remember, when we finished, Bakkies Botha got up and said that he had something to say. Bakkies seldom spoke, but he had a really good ability to talk to the team. He spoke very powerfully to the forwards, saying that we had really let ourselves down.

"His message was that they were resting on their laurels after the World Cup in 2007, that they went through the motions against Wales and didn't pitch the week before in Wellington."

South Africa beat Wales 43-17 in their first test in Bloemfontein, which was also De Villiers' s first as Springbok coach. A week later the Springboks won 37-21, but they had been down 20-21 until 16 minutes before the end.

"I remember that Bakkies was really passionate and emotive. He said, 'We have a decision to make as a team. We should put our faith in Peter. He has picked us when no-one thought we would be picked by this new coach. Are we going to be like other World Cup teams that go through the motions and don't achieve anything more? Or are we actually going to shut everyone up by pitching physically and showing that we have the ability to beat the All Blacks?'

"I came from that meeting thinking it's going to be a bloody tough game, but I felt that for the first time in our tenure there was a real focus."

The few days the Springboks spent in Dunedin prior to the test was an eye-opener to some of the players and coaching staff about the extent of home support for the All Blacks.

Dunedin is small enough for a special atmosphere to be created in the build-up to a game, with shop windows traditionally blacked out. The hype is intensified even further with posters adorning the lamp posts in the streets.

"I've never seen anything as radical as that – not even our send-off to the World Cup in 2011. The country completely rallies behind the All Blacks. Their media, public and the entire propaganda machine supports them. It's very intimidating," says Gold.

But the maturity in the Springbok team – born out of vast experience and World Cup glory – meant the inner belief was there to turn the tables.

They certainly weren't going to allow pre-match hype and passionate student supporters in the university town to impact on them.

Habana also reveals that the team was motivated by the fact that they had been written off. Smit in his own way also contributed, even if he wouldn't be able to run out with the team.

"People weren't even thinking that we had a chance. John sent us a video message the Friday before the game. He mentioned how much he wanted to be there, and how much he as the captain really believed that we could do it under Victor's guidance. And what better opportunity than to do it against New Zealand in New Zealand at a very historic ground," recalls Habana.

"We had nothing to lose. No-one gave us a chance. But there was an utter belief in the side."

According to the wing, De Villiers also gave a good team-talk.

"Peter's a coach who enjoys life and the responsibility of taking charge and being part of something great. He stood up front and said, 'Guys, let's just go out and do this. Let's believe in ourselves. Let's believe in our structures. Let's believe that we can do this. No-one is giving us an opportunity to even come close to New Zealand.'

"That benefited us in a way. New Zealand probably also thought that we were going to fall over and allow them to run riot again."

The first 10 minutes did indeed look ominous as two penalties by Carter gave the All Blacks a 6-0 lead. However, with just over 20 minutes played, Springbok fullback Percy Montgomery's boot had spoken as loudly as Carter's and the teams were deadlocked at 9-all.

Carter edged the All Blacks ahead with another penalty, but South Africa's answer came with the first try of the game.

Centre Jean de Villiers broke superbly before the Boks were ushered into touch in the All Blacks' 22-metre area. The All Blacks then made a mess of the lineout, which gave the Springboks a scrum in a great position.

Joe van Niekerk picked the ball up at the base and attacked on the blind side. The No 8 could have scored himself, but instead passed to wing JP Pietersen, who was over in the right-hand corner.

New Zealand suddenly looked vulnerable and were further unsettled as Springbok flyhalf Butch James slotted a drop goal during a penalty advantage.

But South Africa strayed off-side in desperately defending their line just before half-time and Carter struck his fifth penalty to cut the Springboks' lead to 17-15.

Whatever was said at half-time initially did the trick for New Zealand as they started turning the screws on the Boks.

Sione Lauaki, who had replaced Jerome Kaino at No 8, finished as some slick passing set up a well-deserved try. Carter's conversion made it 22-17 and the momentum swing back in favour of the All Blacks – by now they had scored 10 unanswered points – appeared to offer a winning platform.

But even without Smit, this was a Springbok side that could draw on abundant experience and come the hour mark they had the bit back between their teeth.

A high tackle by substitute back Leon Macdonald on Habana gave James the opportunity to draw the Boks back to 20-22.

However, Carter made the most of a loose pass that smothered a promising All Black attack towards the right-hand side. He grabbed the ball off the ground, spun back to the left and slotted a drop goal that again took the home side out of the reach of a penalty or drop goal.

New Zealand flank Adam Thomson was penalised shortly after the restart for playing a man in the air at a lineout. James's penalty came in off the right-hand post, but they all count.

A little over 10 minutes remained and it was anyone's game with New Zealand carrying a slender 25-23 lead into the home straight.

Then came a moment which really left virtually everyone in the stadium but the Springboks convinced they were beaten.

Matfield was sin-binned for a high tackle with seven minutes left and Carter restored the five-point lead. South Africa would have to play the game out with 14 men and minus their captain.

But scrumhalf Ricky Januarie snatched the unlikeliest of victories with a remarkable bit of individualism. Nothing appeared to be on at the ruck – between the halfway and 10-metre lines in All Black territory – from where he swung his magic wand. Yet he dummied to the left and broke the line before chipping over Macdonald, re-gathering and scoring.

The conversion was left to replacement centre Frans Steyn, who kept a cool head to edge the Boks into a narrow but ultimately decisive lead.

Hearts would nevertheless be in mouths and there would be a final storm to weather before Australian referee Matt Goddard sounded his final whistle.

Carter missed a drop goal to the left and was also crucially brought down by pacey replacement hooker Schalk Brits, who was an astute introduction late in the match after Du Plessis had done the hard yards.

"He just had to shift the ball for the All Blacks to be through, but I dummied as if I was going to take the man on the outside. Carter then held onto the ball and I tackled him on the inside. He makes very few mistakes and that was one of them," recalls Brits.

"Those few minutes I had on the field were some of the toughest I've experienced. The All Blacks tried to hurt me as they cleaned the rucks. They launched attack after attack, but there was a resolve that we wouldn't let this one slip.

"New Zealand have a lot of pace and skill, but as South Africans we also play an effective brand of rugby with our ability to get in people's faces. We're tough guys."

As for Januarie's try, it was the highlight of an international career that might have lasted longer had he looked after his body better.

"It was pure brilliance," says Brits.

"To cap it all, he did it at test level and that makes it very special."

Januarie, who seldom looked particularly interested in media interviews during his career, was pumped up as he spoke just outside South Africa's dressing room shortly after the game.

"We're the number one side in the world and proved it," he told *Die Burger*.

"I looked for space around the rucks throughout the match and eventually spotted a front-row player in front of me. There was another defender in my way after that, so I opted for the chip. Fortunately the ball bounced favourably and I could score the try.

"When I kicked that ball, I thought to myself that the bounce had better be right."

Januarie revealed that the Springboks' defeat at the same ground three years previously – All Black hooker Keven Mealamu scored a late try to condemn them to a 31-27 defeat – had served as his motivation. He also played exceptionally well in that game.

"I thought back to that game in Dunedin in 2005 when the team was announced. It was probably the inspiration for this try. The feeling in our dressing room straight afterwards was awesome," he said.

For just a while the eulogies flowed and De Villiers was the toast of South Africa. He could say what he wanted.

Unfortunately the Boks' world would soon come crashing down.

They finished their tour with a disappointing 9-16 defeat to Australia before thrashing Argentina 63-9 at Coca-Cola Park in Johannesburg in a fixture sandwiched in between the Tri-Nations schedule.

But the gloss was taken off as they were whitewashed 19-0 by the All Blacks in Cape Town and then beaten 27-15 by the Wallabies in Durban.

De Villiers could no longer count on the backing of politicians in the face of the storm. In fact, they wanted him to fail.

It was anticipated with De Villiers's appointment that there would be a strong focus on transformation and that Luke Watson, son of anti-apartheid activist Cheeky, would play a big role in the leadership core of the team.

However, De Villiers appointed John Smit as captain and empowered senior players to help him steer the ship.

Watson started the first three matches under De Villiers – the two against Wales and a victory of 26-0 over Italy at Newlands, as well as the win over Argentina – but was on the substitutes bench in all six of South Africa's Tri-Nations matches.

It would be expensive for Saru to axe the new coach as he had a water-tight contract, but the thought was in any event blown out of the water with a remarkable 53-8 thrashing of the Wallabies in Johannesburg.

Notwithstanding two great victories, South Africa still finished third on the log and overall the campaign was a failure. But it also provided a lasting memory as the Boks stormed the House of Pain in the last game they would play there.

"As much as Ricky's try made the difference, it was a collective effort over 80 minutes that gave us the win. When Victor was yellow-carded the team stuck to the job at hand because the game was there to be won. We had a strong belief that we could still win it with 14 men," says Habana.

"It was great to be part of it. Looking back now, it's a standout game that will be remembered for a very long time."

CHAPTER 16

Routing the Red Rose Army

"Have you seen the expression on Bakkies's face?"
— GARY GOLD TO DICK MUIR

The Springboks love nothing better than beating New Zealand because it represents overcoming the ultimate challenge in world rugby.

But beating England feels almost as good for the simple reason that, as a rule, South Africans generally just don't like them.

So one can just imagine what it feels like to beat the English 42-6. At Twickenham.

It was difficult to envisage the events of 22 November 2008 considering what had gone before it.

The Springboks enjoyed the significant highs of beating the All Blacks at Carisbrook (30-28) for the first time in history and annihilating Australia 53-8 at Coca-Cola Park in Johannesburg.

But those were the sole victories in a Tri-Nations campaign that was perhaps put in perspective by the wooden spoon.

Coach Peter de Villiers's credentials remained in question and he had also lost the backing of politicians who had mistakenly harboured under the impression that he was a puppet on their strings.

Luke Watson was the preferred captain of those who wanted to do the pulling but, irrespective of the circumstances, De Villiers ended up hitching his wagon to John Smit. The old guard of Victor Matfield, Bakkies

177

Botha, Juan Smith, Danie Rossouw, Fourie du Preez, Bryan Habana and Jean de Villiers also remained very much in the picture.

The first two games of the end-of-season tour of 2008 suggested that more trauma would follow the Tri-Nations. South Africa edged Wales 20-15 and then stumbled to a 14-10 win over Scotland.

The Boks, in fact, had even been down 0-10 at half-time against the Scots at Murrayfield.

They could hardly therefore have been considered favourites for the Twickenham clash, especially when one considers that they had won only one of their previous seven matches at England's headquarters.

That was their last encounter there – the 25-14 win that saved Jake White from the sack as Springbok coach.

The losing streak stretched back to 1998 when England ended South Africa's 17-match unbeaten streak and deprived them the opportunity of becoming lone record holders of the most consecutive test victories.

South Africa's 7-13 defeat meant that they had to be content with sharing the former record with the All Blacks.

Cyprus (19 not out!) held the record at the time of writing.

But the biggest humiliation was the 3-53 defeat in 2002 when lock Jannes Labuschagné was sent off in the 23rd minute. It didn't result in much in the line of humility as coach Rudolf Straeuli and captain Corné Krige took a defiant "see you in Perth" line in reference to a pool match they would play against England at the following year's Rugby World Cup tournament. They lost that match 6-25

England had similar raw emotion edging them on after their humiliations at the hands of the Springboks at the World Cup in 2007 and there was much excitement about the direction new coach Martin Johnson was taking.

As if their unflattering record at Twickers didn't provide enough external motivation for the Boks, the English regularly lay it on with pre-match boasting. The lines often heard from their ranks such as "we don't fear them" and "we can match them physically" is simply fuel to the fire of the Springbok belly.

It all sounds a little childish, but is relevant when one considers the credos by which Afrikaners are brought up – "deeds not words" etc.

The result is a deep-rooted sentiment against what is perceived as English arrogance, even though the Red Rose Army's troops are probably being no more than good professionals by talking it up for the sake of lively media coverage.

But it's an approach that is completely alien to South Africa, where the media policy at provincial level is often designed to avoid quotes and head-lines that might "motivate" the opposition.

The Springbok game plan off the field was simple: stay humble, offer no predictions and tell England how good they are. Easy.

Their sincerity would not be doubted as few people outside the South African camp anticipated a Springbok victory in any event.

But behind the veneer there was a strong feeling about what was per-ceived as England's arrogance.

Perhaps it also helped that Springbok coach Peter de Villiers continued to make headlines for his verbal gaffes. In one such instance in the build-up he referred to England flyhalf Danny Cipriani as Danny Capriati (possibly with the women's tennis player Jennifer Capriati in mind).

He said later that it had been by design as part of the psychological warfare. But whether it was by design or not was neither here nor there.

In fact, it helped as it reinforced the perception that the Springboks were an out-of-form side coached by a man whose credentials were in question. England, on the other hand, were supposedly basking in the glow of a bright new dawn. Or so it seemed.

Little did the English know that they were being led into an Isandlwana.

Springbok captain John Smit knew how to tap into his team's psyche

and on the bus trip to Twickenham on game day he made the potentially sensitive request to play the song *Ons Vir Jou Suid-Afrika* – a duet by
Afrikaans singers Bok van Blerk and Robbie Wessels.

De Villiers, who was South Africa's first black Springbok coach, had
no objections and probably saw it for little else than it was – a song from
which the team drew inspiration and fostered a sense of patriotism from
the lyrics.

As it happens, the battle lines very much resembled what went down
in South Africa in the 19th century.

The English were as over-confident as British commander-in-chief Lord
Chelmsford at Isandlwana in 1879 and the Springboks' anger matched
what one might associate with the Voortrekkers at the Battle of Blood
River in 1838.

And, as always, there is a simmering Anglo-Boer War flavour that fuels
public interest in tests between South Africa and England.

As it turned out, the song reached its crescendo as the bus pulled up
at Twickenham and backline coach Dick Muir tapped forwards coach
Gary Gold on the shoulder and asked: "Have you seen the expression
on Bakkies's face?"

The lyrics had no doubt struck a chord with South Africa's lock enforcer, whose sheer physicality often proved a rallying call for team-mates.

Smit had nevertheless left most of his powers of motivation in reserve
for the moments in the dressing room just before the playing of the anthems. He would address the players in the absence of the coaching staff.

Left wing Bryan Habana, who was the International Rugby Board's
reigning World Player of the Year and who was struggling for form at the
time, described Smit's pre-match speech as "heroic".

"John went through every individual and laid claim to what we were
about and wanted to achieve as a side," he said.

Coming off an unimpressive 14-10 win over Scotland, Smit felt that the test at Twickenham had the potential to define the Springboks' year. There had been intermittent successes, but by and large the transition from the old era to the new had proved difficult.

"It had been an iffy year for us and 2008 hadn't panned out as we would have liked from a results point of view. This was our last moment to put a stamp on what kind of year it would be," he recalls.

"As always, it was easy to get guys motivated for a match against England. For some reason I just decided to change things a little. I sat everyone down and went through each player individually. It was a 20-second chat with each guy in terms of what I thought would be pertinent to them in terms of what needed to happen on the day.

"I suppose sometimes you get it right and other times you get it wrong. I think I probably got it right with the majority of the guys that day and they were steaming to get out on the field. They steamed for 80 minutes. It was a *pakslae*."

Adrian Jacobs, who started at outside centre for the Springboks, revealed some of the details of Smit's heroic speech in a post-match interview published in *Die Burger*.

"John really got us going. He took his time and spoke of what he needed from each one of us. The positive energy flowed through the team as a result," said Jacobs.

"He told me that I should do my country proud and that I had made the No 13 jersey my own. I should just keep on doing what I had been doing. It was fantastic to hear that from my captain and to know that I had his unqualified backing.

"He told Bryan that there were a lot of critics, but that we knew what we had in him. John demanded two tries from him.

"He told Ricky [Januarie] that he had been criticised, but that he had done a lot for South Africa.

"Every young player was told that he deserved to be in the team.

"He told Bakkies [Botha] that he could dictate how the match went. Danie Rossouw was told that he had another chance after winning the World Cup for us.

"To Schalk Burger he said, 'Just be Schalk'."

With that out of the way, it was time to do battle.

There was a brief cheer for England as an early penalty by Cipriani put them ahead. But Springbok flyhalf Ruan Pienaar soon equalised as the visitors took complete control.

The first try showcased South Africa's traditional physicality, with flank Rossouw barging his way into a posse of three defenders and carrying them with him as he planted the ball next to the posts.

Not long after that, Pienaar charged down a kick by Cipriani and had a clear run through to score under England's posts.

Pienaar and Cipriani then traded penalties as the match settled into a more predictable rhythm in the second quarter.

The Springboks were also knocked out of their stride a little by a yellow card to loosehead prop Tendai Mtawarira in the 29th minute.

But by half-time South Africa were ahead 20-6 and England would have to score at least three times to take the lead.

It was never going to happen as by now it would have dawned on them that they could not meet the massive challenge they had talked themselves into.

They had neither South Africa's class nor their experience.

And the Springboks were angry.

That anger manifested itself in a ruthless and clinical second half, with South Africa adding three more tries and a penalty by Pienaar.

Jacobs would score next, collecting a delightful off-load by right wing JP Pietersen before breaking the line and rounding his man for the try. England left wing Paul Sackey had come across in vain to try and stop the diminutive Springbok centre from leaving his mark on the game.

South Africa lost fullback Conrad Jantjies to a sin-binning 16 minutes before the end, but England were too shell-schocked to capitalise and normal business was resumed when the Springboks were back to their full staff complement.

Jaque Fourie, who had come on for Jacobs with a little less than an hour played, scored the try of the match with three minutes left. England were attacking close to the Springboks' line in a desperate bid to bring some respectability to the scoreline, but replacement prop Matt Stevens lost the ball in a double tackle by inside centre Jean de Villiers and Habana.

Frans Steyn, who had earlier replaced Pienaar, hoofed the ball downfield and Fourie was on hand to pluck it from under Sackey's nose as it bounced inches before the halfway-line.

England fullback Delon Armitage, whose pre-match words had been particularly prominent in providing the Springboks with their motivation, came across and managed to bring Fourie to ground by briefly getting hold of his ankles.

But the giant Springbok midfielder steadied himself with his right hand shortly before going down. He then spun around before getting up and transferred the ball from under his left arm to his right. Then he used his left hand to keep Armitage at an arm's length before scoring.

Fourie's try highlighted how the Springboks had used their traditional strength of defence as a means of creating play.

The final insult was Habana's try in the left-hand corner right at the end. Prior to that he had been struggling for form, but he latched onto a deft off-load to boost his confidence going into the off-season.

"It was a fantastic game of rugby that no-one anticipated," recalls Habana.

"I had experienced an inconsistent year and it was special to score that final try at Twickenham, where I also scored the first try of my international career.

"To go into the holiday break with a nice win under the belt and having scored the Boks' last try of 2008 was really special for me and helped build confidence going into 2009.

"It laid a good foundation to enjoy the holiday and ensure that the belief inside you never dies. So it was pretty important and crucial that I scored.

"But even if I hadn't scored it would have gone down as a fantastic team performance. Every player from No 1 to 22 made a difference and a contribution that stood us in good stead going into 2009.

"We showed what we could do against the old foe."

Smit highlighted Habana's try as a "nail in the coffin" of the English.

"It was an awesome game to play in and I suppose also to watch," the skipper says.

"We generally played great rugby and there were many exciting moments. For me, my team talk stands out. I remember it as if it was yesterday.

"I celebrated like a little school kid because it meant so much to us to finish the season off well."

Gold believes Fourie's try was such a moment of sheer class that it belongs in a coaching video.

"If you watch footage from the front you can actually see the grass churning up from under his feet," says Gold.

"It was technically an outstanding try and demonstrated what a world class player Jaque is. He's a cut above the rest as a rugby player. It was tickets for England after that try. They were very lucky not to get 50 points against them."

The victory ensured that De Villiers could go into the festive season without persistent questioning of his credentials.

There were understandable concerns among the press and public after the Tri-Nations, but South Africa had completed an end-of-season tour unbeaten for the first time since Nick Mallett coached them in 1997. No-one could argue with that statistic.

The match was a rare occasion where the Springboks' ruthlessness rivalled that of the All Blacks.

South Africa are a different beast to New Zealand in the sense that they are often happy to simply beat opponents rather than thrash them.

"I wish we could have repeated that kind of performance more often," says Gold.

"There were so many occasions where we managed to get ourselves into good positions against Australia and New Zealand, but we seldom 'killed them off'. The All Blacks will in contrast be relentless and continue running at you."

This was one of those intermittent occasions where the Springboks replicated that approach and the outcome was that England conceded more points than ever before in a test at Twickenham.

On reflection, one might say that the new Springbok management didn't get enough credit for what was achieved in 2008.

Fair enough, there had been growing pains. But a 30-28 victory over the All Blacks in Dunedin, a 53-8 thrashing of Australia in Johannesburg and a record victory over England couldn't all be fluked in the same calendar year.

CHAPTER 17

Beasting the Lions

"I don't think I'll ever forget the sight of the Springbok scrum absolutely
obliterating that British and Irish Lions pack."
— BRYAN HABANA

Just what a tour by the British and Irish Lions means to South Africans
was captured perfectly by Springbok assistant coach Gary Gold when he
told the squad of 2009 about the oldest item in his possession: a scrapbook of the 1980 series.

He was one of many boys who at the time collected the pictures of players at the bottom of the now almost forgotten Springbok match boxes.

"I collected every one of them and brought the scrapbook along to show
the players and told them that I was 13 years old in 1980. I have kept it
in spite of moving house numerous times," says Gold.

"The message to the players was how significant our performances
would be. A kid watching a Lions series won't be one anymore when
they return in another 12 years."

It is in that context that the wound that was scratched open by the arrival of the 2009 Lions should be understood.

South Africa, much the better side on paper in 1997, lost the series be-
cause they disobeyed the most basic rule of picking a reliable goalkicker.
They outscored the Lions by three tries to nil in the second test at Kings
Park, but missed all six of their kicks at goal.

The Lions could therefore win the game with five penalties by Neil Jenkins and a famous drop goal by Jeremy Guscott.

It made all the difference when Jannie de Beer was selected at flyhalf for the third test, which the Springboks won 35-16. But by then the horse had bolted and they would have to carry the scar of the series defeat for the rest of their lives.

Interestingly, Springbok coach Peter de Villiers decided to arrange a get-together with the squad of 1997. Such an interaction wouldn't make a great impression on the squad of 2009 because they were young boys in 1997 and didn't carry the baggage of that unnecessary setback.

"We chatted to the team of 1997 about their experience and what it meant to them. They would have to deal with having lost the series in the aftermath and none of them would get the opportunity to play against the Lions again in 2009," recalls Springbok wing Bryan Habana.

"You realise how important it is because it will only come around once in your career."

De Villiers was fortunate to have the significant benefit of adequate preparation time. And, of course, the core of his squad was vastly experienced.

The Super Rugby final was on 30 May and the first test against the Lions in Durban would only be played on 20 June. Lions coach Ian McGeechan would in the meantime run his eye over his squad in their tour matches before picking a team for the first test.

South Africa's biggest headache could potentially have been ring-rustiness. The Bulls' 61-17 victory over the Chiefs in the Super Rugby final was a show of force on their behalf, but a combined Springbok team would have to find its feet in the days leading up to the Durban clash.

The Springboks also had to bond in that period and a creative way of achieving that was turning them into tourists for a day and taking them out to sea to literally swim in shark-infested waters. They were, of course, under the guidance of professionals and didn't face the prospect of being lunch.

But then again, who would not be intimidated by such a scenario with nothing but open shark-infested sea in sight?

"It was about overcoming your fears," Habana recalls about the team-building exercise.

"Some of the guys could have been scared about being 25 kilometres out to sea and surrounded by sharks. It wasn't the easiest thing, so jumping out of the boat was a great sign. You had to overcome mental barriers. If someone was scared we helped him by going into the water and surrounding him.

"You were going out on a limb and realising that, while it wasn't something you did every day, it was fairly easy because you were surrounded by experts and people who backed you up and supported you.

"Not only did we have to grow closer as a team, but we had to trust one another going forward. It was enjoyable and I think it definitely played its part in helping us being successful.

"That could have led to the team getting cohesion and overcoming fears before facing the Lions. If you could face sharks, the Lions couldn't be too bad!"

The Springboks had gathered in Durban on 9 June to start their preparations, which gave them 11 days before the first test – adequate time to ready themselves for the challenge on the field and bond off it.

South Africa's biggest concern was taming the Lions up front and adding to the challenge was the fact that De Villiers had decided to stick with a process he had started on the end-of-season tour the previous year: Picking captain John Smit as tighthead prop rather than in his preferred position of hooker.

The idea was to accommodate both Smit's leadership and the dynamism of Bismarck du Plessis in the starting line-up.

Du Plessis was widely considered the foremost hooker in world rugby and the coaching staff would continuously grapple with the issue of

Smit keeping what was considered a superior player on the substitutes bench.

De Villiers had come up with potentially a great solution as Smit had played prop before, but at the same time there was obviously a reason that he had subsequently focused on playing hooker.

To aid their preparation, the Springbok coaching staff called up forwards from an Emerging Springboks team that was scheduled to play against the Lions on the Tuesday after the first test.

Among the emerging side was experienced Free State loosehead prop Wian du Preez, which would offer Smit stern opposition in a live scrumming session. It made for a fierce training ground battle until the test pack, with Smit at tighthead, managed to get stuck into the rest.

The concern had been that Smit would have to square up to the highly-rated English loosehead prop Andrew Sheridan.

But fate had other plans for Sheridan ahead of the first test. He was struggling with a lower back injury, which meant that Welshman Gethin Jenkins would wear the No 1 jersey alongside the English pair of hooker Lee Mears and tighthead prop Phil Vickery.

Mears was a surprise selection at hooker ahead of the bigger Welshman Matthew Rees. If Jenkins had to be there, it might have been a better option for the Lions to go with an all-Welsh front row of him, Rees and Adam Jones.

The Northern Hemisphere teams, and in particular their media, also tend to believe that their scrumming is superior to that of Southern Hemisphere opponents.

A prominent line of questioning in the build-up to the first test was whether the Lions coaching staff hoped that the referee would "reward the dominant scrum".

Little, of course, did the Lions and their largely sycophantic media contingent realise that it would be the basis of their demise in the first test.

They hadn't factored into their reckoning that their scrum might not be the dominant one.

The Springboks expected Lions forwards coach Warren Gatland to place a heavy emphasis on scrumming and mauling before utilising the platform to shift the ball wide. South Africa prepared accordingly and spent a lot of time working on defence.

Significantly, their preparation with regard to the mauls didn't just focus on how to stop the Lions but also on launching their own drives.

Another selection by McGeechan that played into the Springboks' hands was that of Irishman David Wallace ahead of Wales' Martyn Williams on the flank. It meant that the Lions would play without a specialist openside flank, while the Springboks had drafted in ace fetcher Heinrich Brüssow due to Schalk Burger carrying an injury.

So all in all the South Africans were well equipped for the crucial first test.

They had prepared well and were comfortable in the knowledge that they had beaten Wales, Scotland and England on their end-of-season tour the previous year.

But the pressure was immense as the match in Durban represented the Lions' best chance. The Springboks would potentially be rusty and the match would be played at sea level before the focus shifted to the Highveld.

What is also not commonly known is that the Springbok coaching staff's jobs were very much on the line. The South African Rugby Union (Saru) had made the Lions tour their "get-out clause" for a coaching staff that was continuously viewed with suspicion due to the alleged politics in getting De Villiers appointed ahead of Heyneke Meyer.

If the Lions series was lost, Saru may well have seized on a clause in the coaches' contracts to opt out. Conversely, a series win would suggest that the coaching triumvirate of De Villiers, Gary Gold and Dick

Muir had the qualities needed to take the team to the 2011 World Cup in New Zealand.

The one challenge the coaches wouldn't have was that of motivating the team.

Smit and lock Victor Matfield had briefly abdicated overseas – respectively to Clermont and Toulon – after the 2007 World Cup.

But De Villiers decided to lure back Smit for his leadership, while he also realised that Matfield was without equal as a No 5 lock in world rugby.

The series against the Lions would be the last piece of the jigsaw in the careers of these icons of Springbok rugby as well as that of a number of other senior players. They had won the Tri-Nations and the World Cup, but were entering territory they had not yet and desperately wanted to conquer. This would be their one and only chance.

"I felt more pressure ahead of the Lions series than the World Cup (in 2007). It was incredible because it's just a different kind of pressure that stems from a unique tournament," says Smit.

And, of course, he had the added task of continuing to adapt to playing tighthead prop at test level – arguably the toughest position of all to master.

"It was very difficult," Smit says of the challenge of wearing the No 3 jersey after several seasons as a hooker in the Green and Gold.

"It was nerve-wracking because it's not as if I was going to be coming up against palookas. I was facing some of the best loosehead props in the world.

"What helped me is that I had Bakkies Botha at lock behind me and Juan Smith on the flank. Those two guys provided massive support. The crazy thing is that I only ever received one nomination as a candidate for South Africa's Player of the Year and that was in 2009!"

Notwithstanding the fact that Smit started at tighthead, the Springboks hardly entered the test with a defensive mindset and inferiority complex at the scrums.

"We decided that the only way to deal with it was to bring our own set-piece and mauling into the game. We focused so much on those things that it gave us massive energy when it went well," says Smit.

South Africa flexed their muscles throughout the first half of their 26-21 victory, with loosehead prop Tendai 'Beast' Mtawarira humiliating Vickery in the scrums.

"The first drive, the first scrum and all the penalties that came from it just led to us feeling superhuman," says Smit.

"I think Beast would have done to anyone what he did to Vickery that day. He was just 'in the mood'. When Beast is 'on', he will destroy anyone. He had been bouncing around in excitement from the Tuesday let alone the Saturday morning after hearing about the much-vaunted Lions scrum."

Habana was a spectator from the wing at set-piece time, but the job that Mtawarira did on Vickery left a lasting impression on him.

"I don't think I'll ever forget the sight of the Springbok scrum absolutely obliterating that British and Irish Lions pack," he says.

South Africa's set-piece dominance extended to the lineouts and their first try – scored by Smit in the fifth minute – highlighted some of the team's best qualities.

Fullback Frans Steyn switched the pressure to the Lions' half with a giant clearing kick after visiting flyhalf Stephen Jones had missed a penalty attempt. The Springboks turned over the lineout and moments later used a scrum as a platform to launch the play from which Smit powered his way over. Flyhalf Ruan Pienaar converted and the Springboks were 7-0 up.

Jean de Villiers then highlighted the team's commitment and defensive resolve as he got his arm under the ball when any reasonable person would have expected Lions left wing Ugo Monye to score.

Mtawarira's first annihilation of Vickery came in the ninth minute, with the Lions conceding a penalty from which Pienaar made it 10-0.

The scrum was also a handy resource in terms of transferring pressure, with South Africa able to turn over possession deep in their own half thanks to Mtawarira's continued destruction of Vickery. An attack was launched from there and Steyn slotted a penalty to make it 13-0 after Lions flank Tom Croft was penalised for a late tackle on Springbok scrum-half Fourie du Preez.

The only major fault in an otherwise sublime first-half performance was a fluffed lineout in the 23rd minute, which led to a try for Croft that brought some respite for the visitors. Centres Jamie Roberts and Brian O'Driscoll had combined superbly in the build-up.

Roberts broke the line and off-loaded to O'Driscoll, who cut inside and in turn off-loaded to Croft. Jones converted and the Lions were within striking distance at 7-13.

However, Vickery could again not handle Mtawarira's pressure in the 32nd minute and Pienaar made the score 16-7 from the penalty that the Lions conceded at the scrum.

The Springbok flyhalf then increased the lead further after the Lions were penalised at the breakdown and South Africa led 19-7 at half-time.

Adam Jones was sent on to replace Vickery in the 45th minute, but the Springboks continued their dominance.

First they humiliated the Lions with a maul of over 20 metres upfield. The visitors had no other choice than to transgress and Pienaar then put the ball out in their 22-metre area. There the Springboks set up a second rolling maul from which Brüssow scored. Pienaar's conversion made the score a staggering 26-7 with more than half an hour left.

South Africa had the opportunity to inflict a humiliating and confidence-sapping defeat on the Lions. But the test ended up almost being lost in the Springbok coaches' box.

Sensing that it was in the bag, De Villiers sent on a flurry of substitutes that disturbed the Springboks' rhythm over the course of the second half.

First it was Danie Rossouw for Brüssow in the 52nd minute. Andries Bekker and Jaque Fourie then followed for Bakkies Botha and Jean de Villiers, respectively, in the 57th minute.

Another round of substitutions followed 15 minutes before the end, with Gurthrö Steenkamp and Deon Carstens on for Mtawarira and Smit, respectively. Morné Steyn was also sent on as a blood replacement for Pienaar.

It was just three minutes later that the trio of Roberts, O'Driscoll and Croft combined in a similar manner as before to give the Lions a modest glimmer of hope with 12 minutes left.

But they were still down 14-26 and had no right to win the game.

De Villiers certainly didn't appear to be entertaining the idea and sent on Ricky Januarie to replace the world's best scrumhalf in Fourie du Preez with 11 minutes left.

The Springboks completely lost their way after all the changes, while the Lions had the bit between their teeth.

Morne Steyn made a try-saving tackle on Monye in the 72nd minute, but scrumhalf Mike Phillips was over the line three minutes later to set up a nerve-wracking finish for South Africa.

The momentum had shifted completely and the Springboks were holding on for dear life without much of their leadership core on the field.

South Africa ultimately resorted to cheating. Realising that the situation had spiralled out of control, the message was sent that Carstens should fake an injury so that Smit could get back on.

The skipper returned with three minutes left and the Springboks just managed to weather the onslaught.

South Africa 26, Lions 21.

While the Springboks led the series 1-0, the Lions' morale had been boosted by their performance in the second half and they weren't a dispirited bunch going into the week of the second test.

There was some honest reflection in the Lions camp, with scrumming coach Graham Rowntree telling media on the Sunday morning that he had no reason to dispute the way New Zealander Bryce Lawrence had refereed the scrums.

The Lions' only response could be a change of personnel.

McGeechan beefed up his pack significantly for the second test at Loftus, with Rees and Jones replacing Mears and Vickery in the front row.

There would also be a Lions test debut for 35-year-old lock Simon Shaw, which was a clear sign that the tourists were looking to counter the Springboks with some physicality of their own. Shaw had toured South Africa with the Lions in 1997, but didn't play in a test.

He had subsequently evolved into one of world rugby's most physically imposing players and could best be described as the English equivalent of Bakkies Botha.

Monye's two fluffed opportunities over the Springbok try-line saw him make way for Luke Fitzgerald on the left wing, while Rob Kearney replaced the injured Lee Byrne at fullback. South Africa made only one change to their starting line-up, with a fit-again Burger replacing Brüssow for what would be his 50th test.

Brüssow remained in the match-day squad as De Villiers gave himself the luxury of five forwards on the substitutes bench. There was no need for Januarie as Ruan Pienaar could simply move to the base of the scrum if Fourie du Preez was injured or Peter de Villiers wanted to make a tactical substitution. That allowed the coach the luxury of expanding his forward options on the bench.

Steenkamp was also replaced on the bench with a hooker in Chiliboy Ralepelle. Replacing a prop with a hooker, particularly when Smit and Du Plessis were both in the starting line-up, was a curious decision.

One would have thought the lesson with substitutes would have been learned. Getting the selection and timing of substitutions right is such an integral part of the modern game.

Sheridan, meanwhile, had been declared fit and was named on the Lions' bench.

The Loftus test ended up being a ferocious physical clash before the Springboks prevailed.

This time the Lions scrum more than stood its ground, but both Jenkins and Jones had to be operated on the same night. Jenkins had suffered a cracked cheekbone and Jones a serious shoulder dislocation.

And not all the panel beating in this match occurred within the rules.

Burger, in fact, was later banned for eight weeks for having fingers in Fitzgerald's left eye. However, in the match itself it only translated into a first-minute yellow card, which obviously gave rise to a sense of injustice in the Lions camp after Morné Steyn's last-gasp penalty condemned them to a series defeat.

While he would only be absent for the first 10 minutes, Burger's yellow card was a huge disruption to what the Springboks had plotted for the early stages of the test.

"We did well in the first test in Durban because there was an amazing pace to our game. The focus the entire week before the second test was to start well, go through the phases accurately, hit the rucks, get clean ball and literally start like a house on fire," recalls Smit.

"Schalk then got the yellow card in the first minute and the entire week's preparation had gone up in smoke. Now the focus had to be on slowing the game down to get the 10 minutes out of the way. It was a massive adjustment to make."

The Lions seized the opportunity presented by Burger's absence, with flyhalf Stephen Jones opening their account with a penalty before setting up a try for Kearney with a great off-load in contact.

They were up 10-0 after just eight minutes. But South Africa hit back five minutes later after Burger had returned. Right wing JP Pietersen touched down after a planned move from a lineout and the score was 10-5 to the Lions.

A further penalty and drop goal increased the Lions' lead to 16-5 before Frans Steyn calmed Springbok nerves slightly with a penalty just before half-time.

Jones then restored the 11-point lead and, with less than 20 minutes to go, the Springboks were staring down the barrel at 8-19 down.

But the injuries had brought about the variable of uncontested scrums, which meant South Africa had a comfortable base from which to release Habana for the splendid try that sparked the fightback.

Steyn then added a penalty on top of the converted try and suddenly the Boks were very much in it with 12 minutes left at just 18-19 down.

Jones, however, struck a penalty that put the Lions out of reach of a three-pointer and with 10 minutes left they still very much held the upper hand.

South Africa struck back with what was later voted as the International Rugby Players Association's Try of the Year. Jaque Fourie finished off splendidly in the right-hand corner after the ball had travelled swiftly down the line. The big Springbok centre powered his way through the Lions' replacement flyhalf, Ronan O'Gara, while Phillips also tried in vain to tackle him into touch.

Morné Steyn held his nerve to convert and the Springboks were now in the driving seat at 25-22 up with five minutes to go.

Jones levelled the score with another penalty three minutes before full-time, but South Africa were handed an opportunity to win it when O'Gara clumsily challenged Du Preez while he was in the air.

The kick was 53 metres, but Morné Steyn could fetch that distance on the Highveld and has never been a bundle of nerves. He calmly slotted the penalty to give South Africa the series victory they had craved after the hurt of 1997.

Final score: South Africa 28, Lions 25.

"Thank goodness for Ronan O'Gara," says Smit.

"Rather than kick the ball out to keep the series alive, he launched an up-and-under, chased it and smashed Fourie out of the air. Morné then stepped up for that monster of a kick on his home ground. I don't think I have ever been as nervous in my life (as before Steyn's kick) and so relieved when it went over. I couldn't watch, so I waited to hear the crowd's reaction.

"It was a huge turnaround. People don't understand the character and resolve we had to show after we had the opposite of the start we had anticipated. We started horrendously and the Lions were all over us in the first half.

"It was the most physically intense test I had played in."

To Habana, the test stands out as "one of the classics and one I'm unbelievably grateful to have been a part of".

"The Lions came not only with a fair amount of raw emotion, but also with great players. It led to a physical battle up front and at the back. You look at all 110kg of Jamie Roberts at inside centre and realise it will be tough. Look at the way Jaque Fourie bounced Ronan O'Gara on the way to his try. It was an immensely physical game.

"I'm not too sure what went through Ronan O'Gara's head when he took Fourie out. He will unfortunately have to live with that."

With the series decided, the rest of the Lions tour turned into a battleground off the field. The Springbok camp was very aggrieved at a two-week suspension handed to Botha for charging into Adam Jones at the side of a ruck.

It was a legitimate cleaning of a ruck in the eyes of the South Africans, but was deemed dangerous.

Sheridan even expressed the view from the Lions camp that Botha had been harshly dealt with and perhaps the fact that Jones suffered a dislocated shoulder had played a role in the guilty verdict.

The rage in the Lions camp centred on Burger and the public support he received from De Villiers after the match.

As the debate continued, there were allegations from the Lions camp that De Villiers had endorsed eye-gouging by defending Burger after the match.

De Villiers was publicly slammed by O'Driscoll before the Irish centre flew home with concussion ahead of the third test. O'Driscoll went as far as saying that De Villiers had brought the game into disrepute.

The argument then shifted to whether McGeechan had congratulated De Villiers after South Africa's series victory.

Behind the scenes there were also political tensions brewing. South Africa had won the series and for the dead rubber politicians wanted a team that more accurately represented the country's racial make-up.

Their wish was granted, while some white players also benefited from rotation in the spirit of giving everyone a chance of playing against the Lions.

The starting line-up contained four black African players in Ralepelle, wings Jongi Nokwe and Odwa Ndungane, and the Zimbabwean-born Mtawarira.

Zane Kirchner was also drafted in for his test debut at fullback in place of Frans Steyn. Nokwe and Ndungane were in for Habana and JP Pietersen.

Ralepelle was picked ahead of Du Plessis which, when added to the suspensions of Burger and Botha, meant that South Africa had lost arguably their three toughest forwards. The latter two were replaced with Brüssow and Johann Muller.

Wynand Olivier and Fourie were picked to replace Jean de Villiers and Adrian Jacobs as the centre pairing, while Morné Steyn's match-winning cameo at Loftus was rewarded with a start in the No 10 jersey in place of Ruan Pienaar. Ryan Kankowski also replaced Pierre Spies at No 8.

If the selection pointed to the Boks not being serious enough with their approach to the third test at Ellis Park in Johannesburg, an armband-protest against the suspension of Botha confirmed it in a comprehensive 9-28 defeat.

While the players had the blessing of South African rugby's official-dom, the bosses hadn't anticipated that the white armbands would have "Justice 4 Bakkies" written on them.

A furious International Rugby Board instituted disciplinary steps. An independent committee rapped Saru over the knuckles to the tune of £10,000, Smit had to cough up £1,000 and the rest of the players were fined £200 each.

But that little drama won't be much more than a footnote in the history of rugby union. The fact that South Africa won the series will be much more than that.

The pain of 1997 had been banished.

A Springbok Black-Lash

"It was an intense game that symbolised everything that matches between
South Africa and New Zealand are about. It was uncompromising, hard,
physical, enthralling and exciting."

– BRYAN HABANA

It's probably unfair to compare Springbok teams from over the years because rugby is constantly evolving and by its nature is a work in progress.

But if we narrow it down to the post-isolation phase, we'd probably
arrive at the conclusion that the class of 2009 that triumphed against the
British and Irish Lions, and then went on to win the Tri-Nations, was
right up there.

Of course, the team that won the World Cup in 1995 will probably never cease to be the most famous. But while they beat New Zealand in the
final, it's a fixture they would probably have lost four times out of five.

The core of South Africa's team of 2009 had won the World Cup two
years previously and the likes of John Smit, Victor Matfield, Bakkies
Botha, Schalk Burger, Fourie du Preez, Jean de Villiers, Jaque Fourie,
Bryan Habana and Frans Steyn were ready to step it up to another level.

A series against the British and Irish Lions was all the motivation they
needed and they delivered. Now the Tri-Nations arrived and the chance
was there to prove beyond any doubt against Southern Hemisphere rivals that they were the top side in the world.

The view had been expressed that South Africa were the world champions only because they didn't have to play against other top sides at the
World Cup in France in 2007.

Springbok coach Peter de Villiers had also blooded the likes of loose-head prop Tendai Mtawarira, flank Heinrich Brüssow and flyhalf Morné Steyn to freshen up the squad and give the team some impetus.

By the time the Tri-Nations arrived the Springboks were in the best mental zone imaginable. The confidence was oozing out of them after having beaten the Lions and training sessions were going like clockwork.

But, of course, the true measure is always against New Zealand. The All Blacks were due to defend their status as the International Rugby Board's top-ranked side against the Springboks in Bloemfontein.

Significantly, the Kiwis were without the world's best flyhalf in Dan Carter. Stephen Donald would deputise and he never looked the part.

As it turned out, the Springboks were comfortably better than the All Blacks and would have won more emphatically than 28-19 had it not been for flyhalf Ruan Pienaar missing four out of five kicks in the first half.

Notwithstanding that, the Springboks led 14-3 at the interval. Morné Steyn was introduced for the second half after Pienaar had suffered an ankle injury.

Steyn never looked back for the rest of a memorable tournament. His weak tackle did let in All Black centre Conrad Smith for a try that drew the All Blacks back within seven points after the visitors had trailed 3-17 early in the second half.

But Steyn's temperament proved crucial as he lined up three pressure penalties in the second half.

South Africa gained a decisive advantage eight minutes before the end after the All Blacks' replacement scrumhalf, Piri Weepu, had squandered possession with a wild pass. Springbok flank Juan Smith pounced and then passed to outside centre Jaque Fourie, who raced away for the try.

New Zealand were eating away at South Africa's lead before that and had turned 3-17 into 16-20.

But Fourie's unconverted try meant the visitors were at least two scores down and chasing the game with little time left.

Donald brought the Kiwis within a converted try of a victory with a penalty five minutes before full-time, but Morné Steyn had the final say with a penalty two minutes before the end. It shouldn't have been that close.

The highlight on an individual level was the performance by Brüssow, who won his breakdown duel with All Black skipper Richie McCaw.

Needless to say, the Springboks' confidence soared on the back of the result and there was no fear as they headed to Durban for the second test.

The beauty – or lack thereof as much of the rest of the rugby world was concerned – was the simplicity of South Africa's strategy. Much of it was built around scrumhalf Fourie du Preez's pin-point high kicks that wings Bryan Habana and JP Pietersen revelled in chasing.

Brüssow and hooker Bismarck du Plessis had also added an immense breakdown presence to a team with the best lock pairing in the world in Botha and Matfield.

Du Preez, Fourie and Habana were also at the top of their game. And, of course, Morné Steyn had been added to the cocktail. His debut season was the stuff of fairy tales.

Having struck the penalty that secured South Africa the series against the Lions earlier in the season, he achieved another remarkable individual feat as he scored all South Africa's points in a memorable 31-19 victory in Durban.

Steyn's 31 points were made up of eight penalties, a try and a conversion.

There were other significant milestones. Smit set a world record with his 60th test as captain, while Habana and De Villiers gained their 50th caps.

While South Africa were ultimately utterly dominant, they found themselves on the back foot in the early stages and were down 3-10 after 13 minutes following All Black lock Isaac Ross's try.

It also didn't help that Pietersen got himself sin-binned during the course of the first half, but that was cancelled out shortly afterwards by a yellow card for Ross.

South Africa were down 12-13 with a touch more than 30 minutes played before gaining the initiative when Morné Steyn broke close to the All Blacks' line to score.

The Springboks were up 22-13 by half-time and not even a yellow card for Botha during the course of the second half took them out of their stride.

McCaw was generous in his praise afterwards, saying that it was one of the best Springbok teams he had played against.

The two victories put the Springboks in pole position in the Tri-Nations, with three tests against the Wallabies – in Cape Town, Perth and Brisbane – to come before concluding the campaign against New Zealand in Hamilton.

Steyn scored another 24 points as South Africa beat Australia 29-17 at Newlands before the Springboks headed for their tour of Australasia.

By now, criticism of their supposedly dour but effective game plan was reaching a crescendo. The Springboks took it in their stride, but imagine the surprise and egg on their critics' faces when they produced some splendid attacking rugby in the first half of their 32-25 victory in Perth.

The fresh approach had clearly taken the Wallabies by surprise.

South Africa were 12-0 up after 10 minutes following tries by Du Preez and Fourie. Habana then scored the first of his two tries in the 32nd minute and South Africa led 22-6 at half-time.

They were cruising at 32-13 in the 68th minute after Steyn had added a penalty on the back of Habana's second converted try.

The Wallabies battled back with tries by flyhalf Matt Giteau and right wing Lachlan Turner to give the scoreboard some respectability, but they had been second best by some distance.

Perhaps it was the relative ease with which the Springboks won that sowed the seeds for a comprehensive 6-21 defeat to the Wallabies in Brisbane. The players had treated themselves to some late nights and it showed.

The Tri-Nations would therefore go down to the wire in Hamilton.

South Africa prepared on Australia's Gold Coast rather than jet into New Zealand straight away.

As is his way, Peter de Villiers caused a bit of a stir with a pre-match comment in which he suggested that Hamilton was a boring city. It didn't go down well with the Kiwis, but seldom had a truer word been spoken!

Of course, some things are best left unsaid . . .

Having seen off the All Blacks twice at home and beaten Australia in two out of three tests, the Springboks were craving victory on New Zealand soil.

"The two victories over the All Blacks at home don't stand out as much as the one in Hamilton," says John Smit, who captained the side.

"We were so confident after the series win over the British and Irish Lions that we knew we could do well at home. It was an away victory over New Zealand that we were desperate for and needed.

"We were able to convert the pressure we put on teams at the time, so it was hard for opponents to stay with us."

One of the major challenges the Springboks faced in Hamilton was Carter's return to the All Black side. It was obvious that he was going to make a big difference.

But the Springboks' preparation was that of a team focused on the goal of achieving greatness. South Africa hadn't achieved three successive victories over the All Blacks in a calendar year since 1949.

The Springbok management put together a presentation on what they believed to be South Africa's 10 best performances in history against New Zealand.

It wasn't so much about winning the trophy as it was about claiming it in New Zealand. The senior core had every T-shirt to wear – they had won the World Cup, a Tri-Nations, they had beaten the All Blacks in Dunedin and managed a series victory over the Lions – but they wanted the thrill of clinching a tournament in the All Blacks' backyard.

The jersey handover the day before the test was done by former captain Bob Skinstad.

"I still remember him coming to me on the Friday and asking what the message was that he needed to convey. I told him just to believe that whatever he said would have an impact on the team," recalls Smit.

"We were at that stage where we have the belief, the team and the momentum in our favour. Now we must take what we want. He brought that into his talk subtly.

"We also had an amazing team meeting beforehand where Peter spoke very well. The vibe, the music . . . it was all just perfect. I remember the song by the Black Eyed Peas with the lyrics 'tonight's gonna be a good night' that was used in the presentation. It had everyone bouncing."

A potential concern was the appointment of Welshman Nigel Owens as referee. He is viewed in some circles as a referee who subconsciously favours home teams.

But Smit dismisses the notion that they saw it as a significant obstacle.

"The attitude was that we'd do whatever it takes – even if it had to be against 16 or even 20 men. Today we don't leave until the job is done."

As fate would have it, South Africa were harshly penalised for obstruction at the first kick-off. But the attitude was much the same as that of the 1995 Springboks when Ruben Kruger's "try" wasn't awarded in the final. There were just a few looks at one another from players who were in perfect sync and they got on with the job.

On an individual level, the Springboks' 32-29 victory on 12 September 2009 will best be remembered for the immense contribution by fullback

Frans Steyn, who struck three long-range penalties in the sixth, 10th and 27th minutes.

The first one drew the Springboks level at 3-3, the second one edged them ahead to 6-3 and the third one increased their lead to 19-9.

Steyn's first kick was the hardest blow as it was launched from South Africa's 10-metre line.

"I could see Richie McCaw's body language. He was thinking, 'I can't go off-side anywhere within 70 metres. How am I going to play?' He had to adapt his game. The next thing that happened is that you virtually didn't see Richie McCaw in that test," recalls Smit.

Habana describes Frans Steyn as a "fantastic individual and unbelievably talented player".

"Sometimes people think he's arrogant, but it's just confidence. It's not that he has a 'don't care attitude'. He just has a total belief in himself," says Habana.

"When John looked around Frans was there within five seconds to make sure that he got the ball in his hands to go for poles. They were three magnificent kicks that turned the tide of the game and kept it in our favour. We wanted the All Blacks to play catch-up rugby."

The Springboks' ability to do that took the All Blacks out of their comfort zone because it's not a situation they are used to. Frans Steyn's kicks were very invaluable in that regard as they contributed nine points that most teams would ordinarily not be able to count on.

A key moment in the first half was a try by Du Preez, who had launched a high kick that All Black right wing Joe Rokocoko failed to field. Bakkies Botha pounced in the ensuing chaos and was brought down close to the All Blacks' try-line. Du Preez then found his way over from the ensuing ruck.

South Africa led 22-12 at half-time and it got worse for the All Blacks 11 minutes after the interval when Jean de Villiers intercepted a pass by Carter and finished under the posts.

The Springboks now led 29-12 and the only positive for the All Blacks was that there was almost half an hour in which they could claw their way back.

Five minutes later the Boks were caught napping when the All Blacks took a tap penalty on the halfway line. Left wing Sitiveni Sivivatu finished after a great run by Isaia Toeava, who had replaced Stephen Donald at inside centre.

Carter then added a penalty and suddenly the All Blacks were just seven points behind with 14 minutes left.

But Morné Steyn struck the decisive penalty nine minutes before the end after All Black fullback Mils Muliaina had been caught in possession and the home side transgressed at the ensuing ruck in their 22-metre area.

New Zealand's resolve nevertheless almost saw them snatch victory from South Africa.

McCaw finished after a cross-kick by Carter in the 79th minute and the All Blacks almost repeated the trick right at the death. But this time the ball went out and Owens blew the final whistle.

It was breathtaking stuff and a test that will go down as one of the classics.

"The self-belief in the side and moments like Jean's intercept and Frans's kicks were phenomenal. Those are the moments you remember because they turned the tide," says Habana.

"Jean's intercept try was against the run of play. The All Blacks were attacking and Carter met the Intercept King in Jean, who went to score under the posts.

"It was an intense game that symbolised everything that matches between South Africa and New Zealand are about. It was uncompromising, hard, physical, enthralling and exciting. I don't think there was ever a dull moment where you thought the All Blacks or Springboks were going to run away with it.

"The test will be remembered vividly from a South African point of view because we won the Tri-Nations. It was exciting to see John and Victor hold the Tri-Nations trophy and the Freedom Cup (the trophy for which South Africa and New Zealand compete between them).

"It was truly fantastic to be part of a side that achieved greatness in 2009. It's those memories that you will carry with you for the rest of your life."

Peter de Villiers had the final word when a journalist asked him after the match whether they had found something to do in the city.

"Yes," he replied. "We won the Tri-Nations in Hamilton."

CHAPTER 19

A New Generation

"Flo is the kind of player I want in my team. The harder it gets,
the harder he plays."
– HEYNEKE MEYER

The demands on Heyneke Meyer in 2012 didn't render him so much the Springbok coach as it did a crisis manager.

Apart from the fact that his squad only assembled six days before the first test of his tenure against England in Durban, South Africa had almost lost their entire leadership core in the wake of the 2011 World Cup in New Zealand.

Hooker John Smit and lock Victor Matfield – both considered among the foremost leaders in world rugby – played their last games for their country in the 9-11 quarter-final defeat to Australia.

Furthermore, scrumhalf Fourie du Preez and outside centre Jaque Fourie would both move on to Japan, while flank Schalk Burger had suffered a serious knee injury in the early stages of the Super Rugby tournament and wouldn't play for the rest of the year.

Meyer is a stated believer in the principle that a team needs five key leaders to function and he had lost that many with the combined experience of 420 tests between them. Smit and Matfield had 111 and 110 caps, respectively, with Fourie on 69, Burger on 68 and Du Preez on 62.

To put things into perspective: The team that ran onto the field for the first test against England shared 458 test caps.

The coach therefore had to juggle the combined demands of winning and developing a new spine to the Springbok side. And he would have three training sessions and a captain's run before the first test.

Centre Jean de Villiers, who had done a fantastic job captaining the Stormers in Burger's absence, was installed as captain. His chief lieutenants were hooker Bismarck du Plessis, No 8 Pierre Spies and wing Bryan Habana.

It was then left to a combination of design and accident for the Springboks to evolve to a point where we saw the emergence of key leaders – notably flank Francois Louw and hooker Adriaan Strauss – to complement the seniors such as De Villiers and Habana.

A match in which Meyer's plan came together – as much as it could at such an early stage in his tenure – was the one against Australia at Loftus on 29 September 2012. It was the eighth test of Meyer's tenure.

Habana, Louw and Strauss were among the star performers as the Springboks put the Wallabies to the sword.

Up until that point the Rugby Championship had been enormously frustrating for South Africa. The Springboks kicked it off with a 27-6 victory over Argentina at Newlands and failed to get a bonus point for four tries.

But it was the following Saturday's game that was the beginning of difficult times for Meyer. South Africans, accustomed to convincing victories over Argentina, had to watch the Springboks battle to a 16-all draw against the Pumas in Mendoza.

The Springboks then had a frustrating Australasian tour in which they let slip a golden opportunity to beat New Zealand in Dunedin. The Springboks lost 11-21 after seven kicks at goal were missed. Dean Greyling, who was a prop replacement for Tendai Mtawarira, also let the team down badly with his poor discipline.

Apart from the yellow card he got for elbowing All Black captain Richie McCaw, Greyling conceded another two penalties that were converted into points by All Black flyhalf Aaron Cruden.

A week previously, South Africa had also given up a promising position to lose 19-26 to Australia in Perth.

The Springboks therefore returned to South Africa to face an agitated rugby public in the wake of the disappointment in Dunedin.

But, as the criticism grew, so did the Springboks' resolve.

"The pressure we had on us coming home is always going to be part of rugby," says Habana, who ended up scoring a hat-trick of tries in the win over the Wallabies.

"There is pressure from the public and media, but the big thing we pride ourselves on is the pressure we put on ourselves. We knew we had some amazing talent with the likes of Eben Etzebeth and Adriaan Strauss, who had proved his worth as a leader over those last few games.

"The disappointment of drawing against Argentina in Mendoza and letting it slip in the last 20 minutes against Australia and New Zealand was something we wanted to rectify. Mentally, we had to make a decision to come out firing from the word go and keep that going up until the 80th minute."

Louw considered the game as an important one for the team "to put things right" and on a personal level drew motivation from South Africa's cruel quarter-final exit at the hands of the Wallabies at the 2011 World Cup. He played for an hour in that game after replacing the injured Heinrich Brüssow.

"Everyone has something they use to motivate themselves with. I hadn't been on a winning side against Australia before and it was a big motivating factor. The World Cup sticks in South African minds," says Louw.

"I wouldn't say we lacked confidence going into the game at Loftus. We had experienced a very frustrating two weeks in Australasia. It was important to find our feet."

Meyer, often criticised as a conservative coach in spite of his teams scoring plenty of tries, gave his team the order to cast off the shackles at Loftus.

"My order to the team was to 'cut the ropes', forget about the pressure and express themselves," he says.

Having given Johan Goosen two cameos on tour as a replacement for the out-of-form Morné Steyn, Meyer decided it was time to elevate the gifted young flyhalf to the starting line-up.

Goosen's invention helped spark the Springbok attack and their try-scoring tally was opened by fullback Zane Kirchner, who looked anything but the conservative fullback he is generally viewed as. The ball had gone through the hands of scrumhalf Ruan Pienaar, Habana and Goosen in the build-up.

But it was Habana's class and desire that lit up Loftus.

He scored his first try after running an astute line and collecting the ball from scrumhalf Ruan Pienaar to help the Springboks to a 14-0 lead after half an hour's play. The build-up featured a floated pass as well as an astute change of direction in play by Goosen.

With Louw having scored from a rolling maul 14 minutes into the second half, Habana's quick thinking broke the Wallabies' spirit. This time he found Strauss with a quick throw-in and linked with the hooker before turning on his after-burners to the try-line.

His third owed a lot to an outrageous bit of skill by Louw, who dummied beautifully as he held the ball up in one hand before floating a pass out wide like an American footballer.

The score: South Africa 31, Australia 8.

The Springboks could have won by a lot more. They lacked the ruthless edge of a mature side and also missed six kicks at goal. But there's no need to complain when you beat the Wallabies by such a margin.

"That win meant a lot to us. I think the team took a lot from it and developed as a result. It was a turning point for us," says Meyer.

Habana's extraordinary individual performance capped what was a wonderful Rugby Championship against New Zealand, Australia and

Argentina for him in an inconsistent Springbok side. His seven tries marked him as the tournament's leading try-scorer.

He was later crowned as South Africa's Player of the Year and was a surprise omission when the International Rugby Board (IRB) announced their list of candidates for the same award on a global scale.

But the important thing for Habana and South Africa was that he was back to his best after a disappointing 2011. What was particularly noticeable was the force of his desire to make a difference. It spoke of tremendous character and respect for the Green and Gold jersey.

"I felt it was a challenge to get him back to the best. I always thought it would only be a matter of time before he was firing. I could notice him relaxing a little. His hunger had always been there and sometimes he just tried too hard. I gave him some pointers and involved him in the leadership of the team," says Meyer.

But, admits the coach, Habana's best qualities "could not be coached". An example was his magnificent effort in Dunedin in which he broke the line before he chipped, gathered and scored with All Black captain Richie McCaw and fullback Israel Dagg reduced to mesmerised spectators.

"I had a disappointing 2011 and 2012 was always going to be a watershed for me in terms of where I saw myself. Having got Heyneke's backing and with a successful Super Rugby season behind me, my input as a senior Springbok was going to be important," Habana says.

"Everything just worked at Loftus. I rounded off a great team movement for the first try, then there was the one off the quick throw-in, and then finishing after Francois Louw's great NFL-style pass was pretty awesome.

"It was special receiving the man-of-the-match award and seeing that the contribution I made was really important. I rate it as among my best games in the Springbok jumper."

But perhaps the most important selection Meyer made in 2012 was that of Louw, who was overlooked when the coach named his initial squad. The addition of Duane Vermeulen after he had recovered from a knee injury was also an important step.

Louw made his first appearance of the year as a substitute for Marcell Coetzee against Australia in Perth, while Vermeulen made his test debut the same day starting at No 8.

Coetzee was then dropped to make way for Louw for the rest of the season.

It was not so much a matter of Coetzee having played badly – he had, in fact, been one of the Springboks' most consistent performers – but there was a miscalculation of the balance required in the Springbok loose-trio.

Meyer was not sold on the idea of a specialist openside flank to begin with as he argued from statistics in the Super Rugby tournament that fetchers had a tendency to concede more penalties than the number of balls they turned over.

Heinrich Brüssow, who had been so effective in a glorious 2009 season for the Springboks, fell into that category.

But with the passing of time Meyer realised that a man who could do the business on the ground would be important for the side. Louw fitted the bill perfectly as, apart from his fetching ability, he could carry the ball and be used as a lineout option.

"I can always accept that I made a mistake. I didn't say that there wasn't place for an openside flank. I said that referees were very strict at the breakdown in the way they refereed Super Rugby," says Meyer.

"If you looked at the statistics, the openside flanks would concede more penalties than the number of turnovers they created. It's penalties that win and lose games.

"But I was a little naive because the game is refereed differently on the world stage than at Super Rugby level, where teams don't always commit players to the breakdown.

"England flooded the breakdown and turned every one into a fight for possession. I realised immediately that we would need an openside flank.

"I'd like an openside flank also to be able to be involved in the lineouts because ideally you want five jumpers. It makes a big difference if your loose forwards can jump in the lineouts.

"What I liked about Flo is that he could jump, which not many opensides can do. He's a great ball-carrier and is very good on the ground.

"Duane is also pretty good on the ground and the two of them coming in together gave the team a new dimension. They are not the quickest players, but are really good on the ground. So we had two guys who could make a big impact at the breakdowns, but were also big ball-carriers.

"Flo has stopping power as a defender, but what I really look at as a coach is character and he's a very impressive person. He's a great leader. He's the kind of player I want in my team. The harder it gets, the harder he plays. He played a big part in turning our season around."

Strauss also emerged as an important leader after stepping into the starting line-up at hooker after Du Plessis had suffered a serious knee injury against Argentina at Newlands.

One of Meyer's biggest challenges would always be to find a supporting cast for De Villiers as captain and to that end the emergence of Louw and Strauss were vital developments with an eye to the future.

"I believe you need five leaders in your team to be successful. It was very tough for Jean to take over. He did the job with a young Stormers team earlier in the season, but it was more challenging with the Springboks as those leaders weren't immediately apparent," says Meyer.

"I always thought of Adriaan as a very strong leader. He's highly intelligent and was ready to lead when I told him he had to take on the vice-captaincy in Bismarck's absence. I think we succeeded in creating leaders."

Meyer also had to take some bold steps with the introduction of young blood, and the emergence of bruising lock Eben Etzebeth was hugely significant. It meant that there wouldn't be a yearning for Bakkies Botha after the veteran lock decided to go and wind down his career at Toulon in France.

Indeed, Etzebeth showed that he could be a driving force for the Springbok tight five for years to come.

Juandré Kruger made his debut alongside Etzebeth in the first test against England and established himself as a lineout maestro in Andries Bekker's injury-enforced absence.

The fact that South Africa lost no more than one lineout throw on an end-of-season tour in which they played against Ireland, Scotland and England is a pointer to Kruger's intelligence.

He is not the hardest specimen, but being certain of your lineout possession is particularly important in realising the ambition of physical dominance as it opens up opportunities for driving mauls.

There were also some promising signs in Patrick Lambie's performances at flyhalf on South Africa's end-of-season tour. He got his opportunity thanks to Meyer's decision to axe Steyn and an injury to Goosen.

So slowly but surely a team took shape, with an impressive victory over Australia lighting up what was an inconsistent year.

"The team was at a vulnerable stage of transition from the old to the new," says Louw.

"The victory over Australia showed what we were capable of when the team gelled. We showed what the new era could produce."

But as the season wound down and ended with the narrowest of victories over England, one felt compelled to look further than the emergence of a new generation. The veterans had made telling contributions.

A 31-year-old De Villiers was immense as captain. It needed a leader of serious substance to handle the transition and he stepped up in that regard.

In time it may well be recognised as his most important contribution to Springbok rugby as he wasn't able to fully share in the joy of the 2007 World Cup after tearing a bicep in South Africa's opening pool game against Samoa.

He missed the 2003 tournament with a serious shoulder injury and played in the 2011 quarter-final, which the Springboks lost partly as a result of New Zealand referee Bryce Lawrence freezing on the big occasion.

But Springbok rugby is not about writing an individual script and Habana's simply-stated goal should perhaps be the guiding light for anyone who has the incredible honour of pulling over the Green and Gold jersey.

"I want to be able to leave the jersey in a better place than where I received it," he says.

May that always be the mantra for future generations as they carry the torch.